Whip Your Career Into Submission

Also by Karen Salmansohn

How to Succeed in Business Without a Penis

How To Make Your Man Behave in 21 Days or Less
Using the Secrets of Professional Dog Trainers

50% Off: A Novel

The 30-Day Plan

to Transform Yourself from a Job Slave

Into the Master of Your Destiny

Broadway Books   New York

Whip Your Career Into Submission

Karen Salmansohn

BROADWAY

WHIP YOUR CAREER INTO SUBMISSION. Copyright © 1998 by Karen Salmansohn.
All rights reserved. Printed in the United States of America. No part of this book
may be reproduced or transmitted in any form or by any means, electronic or me-
chanical, including photocopying, recording, or by any information storage and re-
trieval system, without written permission from the publisher. For information,
address Broadway Books, a division of Bantam Doubleday Dell Publishing
Group, Inc., 1540 Broadway, New York, NY 10036.

Broadway Books titles may be purchased for business or promotional use or for
special sales. For information, please write to: Special Markets Department, Bantam
Doubleday Dell Publishing Group, Inc., 1540 Broadway, New York, NY 10036.

BROADWAY BOOKS and its logo, a letter B bisected on the diagonal, are trademarks of
Broadway Books, a division of Bantam Doubleday Dell Publishing Group, Inc.

Library of Congress Cataloging-in-Publication Data
Salmansohn, Karen.
Whip your career into submission: the 30-day plan to transform yourself from a job
slave into the master of your destiny/by Karen Salmansohn.—1st ed.
p.   cm.
ISBN 0-7679-0181-9 (hardcover)
1. Vocational guidance for women.   2. Businesswomen.   3. Career development.
4. Women—Employment.   I. Title.
HF5382.6.S25   1998
650.14′082—dc21   98-11280
                            CIP

FIRST EDITION

Designed by Claire Vaccaro

98   99   00   01   02   10   9   8   7   6   5   4   3   2   1

Whip it until it's good and stiff.
JULIA CHILD

No, you will not whip me, my dear. It is I who will whip you.
MARQUIS DE SADE

Whip it, whip it good.
DEVO

You've got to stop leaving your career destiny to the
whims of fate—and take a whip in hand.
KAREN SALMANSOHN

The reasonable man adapts himself to the world;
the unreasonable man persists in trying to adapt the world to himself.
Therefore, all progress depends on the unreasonable man.

GEORGE BERNARD SHAW

Dedication

I'd like to dedicate *Whip Your Career Into Submission* to my very first disciplinarians:

my mom and dad.

To be serious for but a moment (and then I promise I'll revert back to my normal nothing's-too-sacred-for-a-little-sardonic-humor mentality) . . . I want to wholeheartedly (from every artery) thank my mom and dad for their consistent and persistent faith in my ability to pursue and snag my career passions—even when these passions have had naughty titles. As you can well imagine, it takes very special parents to support a daughter who writes books with the words "penis" and/or "whip" in their titles.

I love you both.

Acknowledgments

I have four words to sum up what it's like to be a whip smart, sexy, warm, witty, supportive, extraordinary, uncommon woman—with great fashion sense—here in the '90s:

Lydia Wills, Suzanne Oaks

Or make that:

Suzanne Oaks, Lydia Wills

Because when it comes right down to it, I don't know who to thank first.

Lydia is an agent who goes so far beyond the call of duty that I've on occasion slipped and referred to her as "my therapist."

And Suzanne is that rare kind of editor who knows how to crack that whip—and make you love her for it.

I'd also like to send my deepest appreciation to the good-humored Ann Campbell, and the good people at the Space Untitled Cafe who kept pouring me coffee after coffee while I pored over the pages of this book.

I'd also like to thank that one and only special soulmate man in my life—who generously supplied the whip seen on the cover from our home collection (just kidding).

Okay. Now here's the part where I list a very, very, long barrage of names of people who I adore and want to thank. So, pour yourself a cup of coffee (or head to the Space Untitled Cafe in Soho, New York, for some) and read on:

Marisa, Amy, Meryl, Bob, Harvey, Steve, and all the Miramax folks, Bryan, Lauren, Phyllis, Tessa, Margaret, Susan, Suzanne, Suzanne (no, that's not a typo. I just know a lot of Susans and Suzannes), Jay, David, Mark, Robin, Tommy, Madonna (just trying to impress you), George Clooney (just trying to get on his good side—though all his sides seem pretty good to me), Susan, Pip (yes, that's her real name), Eric (my big brother), Rona, George, Nancy, Pete, Ole, Jon, Jon, everyone at Readers (a fab office supply store on 10th and University), Bob, Jeff, James, Steve, Greg, Tom, Robin, Stuart, Gill, George, Ivy, Gerard, Ben and Jerry's Ice Cream, Jon, Cara, Lori, Eric, Tony, Lee, Neena, Tom (the photographer), Lee, Scott, Marcia, Steffy, Owen, Trevor, Sneezy, Happy, Grumpy, Doc and the rest of the gang (just seeing if you're still paying attention), Colin, Dan, Susan, David, Fran, Carol, Antge, Sing, and a big thank you to Tekserve Computer Repair.

Contents

The Master Plan for Success: An Introduction

How do you feel about your career right now? Is it rewarding? This question's not to be confused with: Does your career *appear to the outside world* to be rewarding? Do you feel like a slave at your job? A slave to circumstance? Do you want out? Do you want up? Do you want a vacation from the meaningless muddle, brainless impulses, and relentless routine that you call your 9-to-5 (make that 8-to-9) life?

If so, you've got to stop leaving your career destiny to the whims of fate—and take a whip in hand. Trust me. Whims won't get you nearly as far as whips. You must learn to become the master of your job destiny—and to do this *you must first learn to become the master of yourself.*

You've got to work from the inside out. In other words, before you can enjoy the fun of controlling your career and others, you *first* must learn to control yourself—*master resisting* those alluring temptresses like worry, fear, anger, cynicism, impatience, stress, and the preference to spend one's time lolling around in a hammock sipping margaritas.

Of course this takes discipline. But in the end you'll find this discipline NOW will lead to much pleasure LATER. For example:

1. The titillation of watching misbehaving, colicky colleagues cower in your presence.
2. The thrill of experiencing disobedient whiny employees begging to satisfy your every command.

3. The overall turn-on of S&M—success and money.

You can attain all of the above once you attain self-mastery. If you cannot master yourself, then you will forever be subjugated by yourself and your negative emotions (like the aforementioned worry, fear, and cynicism), as well as your boss, your colleagues, your employees, your parents, your children, your inner children, your dog, your inner dog—you name it.

Self-mastery is the hardest job you will ever have. But it's the FIRST JOB you must take on *to get the job you truly want.* Hence, the USE OF CAPITAL LETTERS LIKE THESE, and *italicized letters like these*—to remind you how important it is to *FIRST MASTER YOURSELF.*

In fact, THIS is *the main principle of this book*—and it's not so much inspired by the original dictionary definition of S&M, as it is by CEOs, VIPs and Zen. Both Zen masters and Fortune 500 masters agree:

Mastery of your outer world must first begin with mastery of your inner world.

When you discover the power of self-mastery, you will see your world change before your eyes—maybe not all at once, but slowly and steadily—you know, like Jeff Goldblum in that movie *The Fly.*

And speaking of movies . . . The self-mastery secrets you'll find throughout this book are what made *my* world change and what made me achieve my goal—my *dream:* landing a Miramax movie deal.

It's like this: When my novel, *50% Off,* first came out, I allowed my literary agent to serve as my Hollywood movie agent, which didn't serve my book to its fullest advantage. A year later, when I switched agents, I was excited to have a real pro in the film industry to sell my novel to Hollywood. But, to my disappointment, he told me too much time had passed, that I had missed my window of opportunity. I asked if there were some back doors—like maybe sending the book to some actresses his agency represented. He promised he would look into it—but didn't. Then he said he *did* send out my book—but when I asked for specific names, he gave nothing but vague answers.

I was dominated by hopelessness, anger, sadness, regret—pick a negative emotion, any negative emotion. I wished something could be done. After all, if I were my own agent, I wouldn't give up on me.

Then I realized I could be my own agent. Instead of allowing my one big shot at my dream to be handled by someone who obviously wasn't nearly as obsessed as *I was* to make it happen, I could take control of the situation myself. I started asking everyone/anyone I knew who they might know who could help get my novel into the right appreciative movie mogul's hands. I asked this one. I asked that one. Then I asked this one if he knew another that one.

Months passed. Then another year—and my novel still was not sold. But I remained fiercely determined. I was like one of those cockroaches that you keep spraying, spraying, spraying with insecticide, but just won't die. The last survivor of a nuclear war. That was me.

One evening I went to see a play at a theater troupe in town called Naked Angels, of which, I noticed, actress Marisa Tomei was an active member. I had always respected her ability to portray funny, feisty, sexy, smart women—qualities that my novel's protagonist would offer an actress the opportunity to play. The next day I asked my agent to send her my novel. Again, he told me: Give up. Chill out. It's too late.

I almost did.

But something in my head just clicked—or maybe that was the sound of that career whip cracking. ANYWAY . . . I dropped off a copy of my novel on my own to Marisa over at Naked Angels. Eight months later I received a call. She wanted to option my novel.

The lesson?

Instead of leaving a career dream up to the whims of fate,

*it's essential to take that whip in hand and become the domina-
trix of your destiny.*

It is from my own firsthand experience with wielding that
career whip that I'm encouraging you to do the same. Take control. Be in command. Unshackle those limiting negative beliefs.
Do it now and transform yourself from:

a SLAVE to life's circumstances

into

a MASTER of your job destiny.

Plus, consider these other nifty career options that will open
up to you:

You will stop being

a SLAVE who wants and begs,

and you will become

a MASTER who chooses and acts.

You will stop being

a SLAVE who dies on your knees,

and you will become

a MASTER who fights on your feet.

You will stop being

a SLAVE who hears "No way!"

and you will become

a MASTER who hears "Know the way!"

You will stop being

a SLAVE who complains "Not again!"

and you will become

a MASTER who promises "Never again!"

You will stop being

a SLAVE who becomes *The Little Engine That Could—
But Didn't,*

and you will become

a MASTER who becomes *The Big Steamroller Who Does It All.*

You will stop being

a SLAVE who is always getting corner time,

and you will become

a MASTER who is always getting the corner office.

You will stop being
a SLAVE who says: God hates me, why bother, my career life
is a veritable obstacle marathon, with flaming hoops, hidden
sand dunes, and demonic, smiling clowns with hidden buzzers
in their palms who are just waiting to shake MY hand,
and you will become
a MASTER who says: Oh cheer up, goddamn it!

What separates the Master Mentality from the Slave Mentality is but one small thing—a thing called CONSCIOUS THOUGHT—which leads to another crucial thing called CONSCIOUS ACTION. To develop this Master Mentality over conscious thought and action takes time—but not too much time. I believe you can master it in 30 days. In fact, psychologists say a habit takes 21 days to kick in. So I'm throwing in an extra nine days to make sure your new Master Mentality habits get kicked into you just that little bit stronger and harder.

I believe the same way your body can be strengthened, your mind can be, too. You just have to work at it. If you want to increase your biceps, exercise them. If you want to increase your conscious thought—exercise it.

I did. And do.

I've worked hard at controlling my thoughts. It hasn't been easy. You know how it's good to try to be the best you can possibly be at a particular skill? Well, I unfortunately learned how to be *the best at being neurotic.* I used to be Olympic level at second-guessing—and third-guessing—and one-hundred-and-third-guessing myself. Although, thank God (and those acting classes in high school), this habit never truly showed to the outside world—or did it?

I once had a psychic tell me: "You are a perfectionist."

My response: "No I'm not. I'm not nearly a perfectionist enough."

It wasn't until after those words left my lips that I realized how . . . well . . . *neurotic* I sounded.

Thankfully I'm now a recovered neuroticaholic. Ultimately I realized: *So many neuroses, so little time.* If I truly wanted to go far in my career, I couldn't let my neuroses hold me back. So I devised ways to control them instead of allowing them to control me—and reaped satisfying results.

I want the same for you.

I personally know how hard it is undoing all those years of effort it takes to become a superior neurotic. It took me a lot of discipline. It took me a lot of work. It took me a lot of tears. It took me a lot of massages with this wonderful Swedish woman named Antje. But in the end, it paid off—and even paid for those massages with Antje by earning me a nice, plump income—even after I quit my senior VP ad gig at age 27 to write my novel.

After I quit my job, I worried that I'd never be able to match my six-figure income in the years to come. But I knew that I hated working my butt off, being tortured by tyrannical bosses and seemingly clueless clients. At least if I quit, I had a chance to be tortured in a new, more creatively satisfying way.

Unshackled from the chains of my long hours/little satisfaction life in advertising, I began a freelancing assignment at MTV writing promos (those little 30-second spots that run between videos). One day I was heading home when Mark, this talented director, joined me at the elevator bank. I had met him once before through mutual friends, and wanted to talk with him. He was always working on cool, interesting projects and seemed like a valuable business contact—as well as a sweetie of a guy.

We got on the elevator together at floor 24. For the first few floors heading down, my neuroses took over. I started thinking:

I should say hi. But what if he doesn't remember meeting me? He's so successful and talented—what if he snubs me? Or thinks I'm too pushy? What if I make a goofball of myself? Why am I wearing this god-awful dress? Why would anybody want to talk to anyone who would wear a god-awful dress like this? Plus, he's probably stressed out and not in the mood to talk. As am I. What a grumble-grumble day. Between the stress and this dress, I am doomed to live a life of failure. Just shoot me now.

Then on about floor 18, I became conscious of my automatic negative, neurotic thinking. On about floor 15, I started telling me: Fuck it. You miss 100 percent of the career opportunities that you never go for. Fear of being a loser can keep you from becoming an anybody. And I'm at least an anybody—if not a somebody. After all, I'm a kind, talented, established writer— and the type of girl who can get away with wearing a god-awful dress like this—even make it look damn good. Of course he'll want to talk with me.

"Hi," I said to him on floor 12, "Remember me?"

He did.

By lobby level he had given me his agent's number and address to send my novel. And that's how I got my first agent and first book sale. It's a good thing MTV was located on the 24th floor and not the third floor or I might never have been published. And it's a good thing I took control of my negative thinking through *conscious thought.*

Time and time again I was witnessing that the more balanced and together I could remain on the inside, the more balanced and together my career life was becoming. In fact, using these "balancing act secrets" that I will reveal up ahead, I was able to turn MTV's initial rejection of a TV show pitch that I gave them into a positive, lucky break. I reformulated the original show that was rejected so as to be positioned for a younger Nickelodeon audience and sold the show there. Meanwhile, I was keeping in touch with my "rejectors" at MTV—dining with them—without whining with them. Soon they asked me to come back and pitch again—and a *second* TV deal was made.

But all of this positive conscious thought leading to positive conscious action did not come easy. It took work at developing my mental discipline, until it became instinct.

There's a famous quote:

"According to your faith, be it unto you." (Matthew 9:29)

There's also a not so famous quote:

"When you master conscious thought, you can control your faith and thereby control your destiny." (Karen 9:29 A.M.—just written this morning).

In the pages ahead I will offer humorous, yet fiercely serious, effective exercises and techniques that will help you take your conscious thought from weak to peak levels, by helping you build a muscular, powerful, throbbing, brawny brain that will be strong enough to break those chains of negativity. Plus, I will show you how to train your brain to tap into powerful reservoirs of energy, joy, satisfaction, higher self-esteem—even improved physical health.

In the same way some yogis can master their heartbeat through conscious thought, you will soon learn to have self-mastery over your restraining beliefs—until this Master Mentality becomes second nature.

I promise you that by your 30th day, you'll find that what started off as mental discipline will no longer feel like discipline. You might even start to see it as something to look forward to—something fun. You'll be surprised by how indulging in discipline can actually bring you to the highest emotional highs—often to be followed by the highest tax bracket. After all, winners are just disciplined thinkers, folks who have learned to control their thoughts, instead of the other way around. You know Oprah Winfrey? She was into discipline. Helen Keller? Mother Teresa? The ultimate dominatrixes. But I'm skipping ahead to Principle #8 of my Master Plan for Success that I invite you to read every morning— make that: *I COMMAND YOU TO READ EVERY MORNING, DAMN IT.*

As you can tell by my above whip-cracking attitude—as well as my choice of BOTH italicized and capitalized typography—I mean business. And I believe that reading my Master Plan daily will help you improve whatever business you're in. By devouring healthy, powerful mental thoughts first thing in the morning, you'll gain the mental energy needed to make it through even the most stressful, challenging business day. So, for the next 30 days I want (aka *COMMAND*) you to start your day by reading the following:

The Master Plan for Success

Principle #1
If you're gonna whip a career—whip your own career.
Don't whip somebody else's.

If you're going to spend your time and energy whipping, you must first find a career that will turn you on—not turn on your mom, your dad, your boyfriend, your landlord, your manicurist. You must always mix self-pleasure with business.

Principle #2
To find a career worth whipping, you must
first remove that leather hood, so you can clearly see
who you really (really) are.

We're all like Superman/Clark Kent—with one big difference. In public we walk around in our Superman outfit playing a super-hero, and in our secret identities, we are really Clark Kent. The problem is most of us spend too much time trying to make our capes flashier and trying to become objects of envy to cowork-ers—attempting to brandish super power by flinging our color-ful capes in each other's faces. Meanwhile, it's our weak, Clark Kent selves that really need the strengthening for us to gain true super power. Unfortunately, sometimes this hidden Clark Kent identity is a secret we even keep from ourselves. To become pow-erful (and powerfully happy) you must FIRST acknowledge this self—and its power—*its secret career whip-wielding weapon.*

Principle #3
What keeps you in chains are your self-limiting
thoughts. You must unshackle them to go anywhere.

If you plan to go far, you must first free yourself from the chains that bind you with self-fulfilling limiting expectations. When you remove these limitations (e.g., "I'm too old to switch tracks," or "That career is too competitive," or "Maybe I should just stay where I am for another year," repeated over and over again for a decade), you will find the work world offers you unlimited opportunities that flow nonstop—like that scene in *Fantasia* with Mickey and all those slobbering buckets of water. Believe and receive.

Principle #4
You must not be a slave to your past.

A slave defeatedly and repeatedly blames his childhood for present problems. For example, a slave says: "My childhood was full of pain and poverty, so now my career must be." Whereas a master says: "Childhood shmildhood." (In fact, mine was more of a shmildhood. But that's another story.) Anyway . . . A master knows how to let go, move on—recognizing that although you cannot change past outer events, you can change their present inner interpretations, by rewriting your autobiography to include inspiring character-bolstering lessons.

Principle #5
You must beat all your negative thoughts,
instead of letting them beat you.

The way some people have a drinking problem, others have a thinking problem. They start their day with one negative thought, then they just can't stop. For example: "I suck. My boss sucks. My job sucks. The world sucks. Distant galaxies suck." Basically, by the end of the day they've completely conjugated the verb "to suck." I believe it's important to listen to your career vents—but then quickly put a gag in their mouth.

Principle #6
You must find the pleasure in your pain—
and know that pain is a good teacher.

Slaves have a chain reaction to life's inevitable calamities and even its smaller disappointments—meaning they keep torturing themselves with their insecurities and fears, weakening themselves even further. For example, a slave's reaction to being fired is to beat himself black and blue with that pink slip. Whereas a master becomes a master reinterpreter—and looks for lessons to be learned, bad habits to be spurned, and better jobs to be earned.

Principle #7
You must make sure your long-term goal plays the dominant role in your career.

A master doesn't get sidetracked by subordinate duties. A master always lets the long-term goal dominate. While a slave gets overpowered by bullshit and bullies, a master stays in charge of visualizing and satisfying the big picture.

Principle #8
Discipline can be fun!

Every successful person is into discipline. Ted Turner, Tina Turner, Oprah Winfrey, Madonna, and Mother Teresa are a few of the many who discovered the joy of putting their butts to work and sticking with it—even when their problems—whether being in an abusive relationship or losing millions of dollars in a business venture or coping with general human suffering—seemed insurmountable. In time, discipline can even become addictive. Bad habits are hard to break, but good habits—because of all the wonderful rewards they bring—can soon become a natural lifestyle.

Principle #9
You give someone enough rope, he'll tie you up with it.

You must avoid getting caught up with catfighting employees, dogmatic bosses, and bulldozing colleagues. They deflower your power.

Principle #10
You should never be afraid or guilty or ashamed of the power that you feel when wielding a whip.

Too many people—particularly women people—suffer from *Keeping Down With the Joneses Syndrome*. They feel guilty/insecure about surpassing friends/lovers/family on that climb up the career ladder. A master wisely says: "Fuck guilt and insecurity!"—and instead seeks S&M—success and money.

Principle #11
To be a good whipper, you have to keep yourself in a state of excitement.

Enthusiasm is the fire you need to make sure your burning desires don't burn you out. A master knows that to keep this fire going you need to find a balance of work and play—and to find the play in your work, remain in touch with that primal desire for whipping.

Principle #12
You've got to keep whipping and whipping to make a lasting mark.

The people who make a living doing what they love are the people who insist on it and persist in it—folks who practice HOCUS FOCUS over long periods of time without giving up (e.g., achieving my dream movie deal was a four-year process!). What you focus on constantly with great emotion and expectation eventually has no choice but to become reality.

Principle #13
A master knows the importance of practicing foreplay—I mean fair play.

A master knows how to maintain masterhood while still maintaining humanhood. A master pursues S&M—success and money—with C&GW—*compassion* and *good will.* Believe me, a lot of people in this world—bosses, friends, employees—have probably given you more than your fair share of empathy and support during some trying times. Share the wealth—you'll be amazed how good it feels.

Principle #14
A master knows opportunity doesn't spank—I mean knock—just once. A master knows unlimited opportunity is all around.

A master keeps an open mind, always ready and listening for new projects, jobs, growth opportunities, and networking possibilities. The world is full of people who want to know *you,* too: Make the decision to be assets for one another.

The above principles share something in common with that commercial for Hair Club for Men. Just like that spokesguy, I'm *not only* the spokesgal for the above, I'm also a *"member."* Every morning before I start my day, I remind myself of these principles and thereby rouse myself into a powerful state of mind that gives me the mental strength to dominate over negative thinking, backstabbing weasellike coworkers, and spineless wormy bosses.

What the Thighmaster did for the thigh, I promise you this book will do for your career—offer noticeable improvements, in a short amount of time. Think of this book as your *Careermaster*—which is what you will soon become: a CAREER MASTER.

I promise you that if you commit yourself to this book, by the end of the next 30 days you will definitely find yourself on the correct end of the career whip.

Let's get cracking, shall we?

Mistress Karen's Four Disciplinarian Dictums for Using This Book

You ready? Are you tingling with excitement? This is where the fun and games begin. At least that's how I'd like you to think of the next 30 days. After all, that sounds a lot friendlier than "This is where the painful poking and probing into your tender psyche begins." Okay, here they are . . .

Mistress Karen's First Disciplinarian Dictum

Invest in a journal so you can write down your responses to my exercises and chart your progress. (However, if you wish to rebel against Mistress Karen's command and remain journal-free, so be it. You can simply devote a certain amount of musing time to my questions, and hope for some good memory recall. But your career won't submit to you nearly as quickly. This is not a threat—not that I personally have anything against threats. I'll be doing my share of that with you later. And you'll love it—or else. Anyway, it's just that I have witnessed with myself and my fabulously successful friends the miraculous "I WRITE THERE-FORE I AM" powers of keeping a journal. I truly recommend it.)

Mistress Karen's Second Disciplinarian Dictum

Start your morning by reading my Master Plan for Success. Your goal: become *intimately familiar* with these principles:

PRINCIPLE #1 If you're gonna whip a career—whip your own career. Don't whip somebody else's.

PRINCIPLE #2 To find a career worth whipping, you must first remove that leather hood, so you can clearly see who you really (really) are.

PRINCIPLE #3 What keeps you in chains are your self-limiting thoughts. You must unshackle them to go anywhere.

PRINCIPLE #4 You must not be a slave to your past.

PRINCIPLE #5 You must beat all your negative thoughts, instead of letting them beat you.

PRINCIPLE #6 You must find the pleasure in your pain—and know that pain is a good teacher.

PRINCIPLE #7 You must make sure your long-term goal plays the dominant role in your career.

PRINCIPLE #8 Discipline can be fun!

PRINCIPLE #9 You give someone enough rope, he'll tie you up with it.

PRINCIPLE #10   You should never be afraid or guilty or ashamed of the power that you feel when wielding a whip.

PRINCIPLE #11   To be a good whipper, you have to keep yourself in a state of excitement.

PRINCIPLE #12   You've got to keep whipping and whipping to make a lasting mark.

PRINCIPLE #13   A master knows the importance of practicing foreplay—I mean fair play.

PRINCIPLE #14   A master knows opportunity doesn't spank—I mean knock—just once. A master knows unlimited opportunity is all around.

Mistress Karen's Third Disciplinarian Dictum

Think about each day's career lesson *three times a day*—perhaps even discussing each day's lesson with a friend or paramour (I love that word) at mealtime. By checking in with yourself periodically, you can better spot where/how/when you're tempted to play the role of job slave.

Mistress Karen's Fourth Disciplinarian Dictum

You must decide now—once and for all—that you are 110 percent willing to put in the discipline needed to change your career. And it will take discipline. But know: This discipline *now* will lead to much pleasure and many fantasies fulfilled. I promise. And so does fellow disciplinarian Michelangelo, who confessed, "If people knew how hard I worked to get my mastery, it wouldn't seem so wonderful after all."

To demonstrate your devotion to discipline, I want you to sign the following contract:

I, _____, hereby announce that I am 110 percent committed to the DISCIPLINE necessary to WHIP MY CAREER INTO SUBMISSION. I will always keep in mind that: my FAITH determines my DESTINY. So I will discipline myself to make sure that MY FAITH will remain STRONGER than my fears, doubts, cynicism, anger—any/all of the career subjects I will no longer be subjugated by in the 30 days ahead.

_____
Signature

Whip

Misdirection

Into Submission

or

....

It Doesn't Matter How Fast You Get There, If You're Heading the Wrong Way

....

Just last month, I was rushing on a subway from the Village to the Upper West Side to meet a friend for dinner. Because I was in such a hurry, I didn't take time to read the subway map. I wound up on an express train . . . that was a little too express. Before I knew it, I had gone 60 blocks in the wrong direction.

Too many of us make this mistake in our rush to find a career—and then we remain at our wrong destination, which is the career equivalent of settling for hanging out at a K-mart, because that's where the subway stopped, when you wanted to meet your friend at Taste of Tokyo Sushi Palace. You may be tempted to throw up your hands and stay right where you are. But trust me:

It's better to have a short wrong job
than a long wrong job.

No matter how satisfying the price breaks are at K-mart, they still won't fill that craving in your belly for tuna sushi rolls.

For instance, I originally arrived in advertising as a profession because I thought it would be glamourous, cool, and exciting, and I'd get to be creative. Eventually, I found all that fluffy glamour stuff thoroughly unsatisfying. Basically, I was being given the opportunity to afford to wear expensive, gorgeous clothes while having to write embarrassing, vapid, soulless TV spots.

Pussy Talk

I remember once I was working on creating the Purina Cat Chow jingle of the nineties. I was told that I could only use a three "chow, chow, chow" hook, because that was what was trademarked. Two chows weren't. I could, however, use four chows, as long as that fourth was close enough to the first three in rhythm to feel like a three-chow/one-chow. After the jingle was produced, the client and I debated in long, drawn-out meeting for days—and weeks—and months—whether the hook I ultimately created was a "two-chow" or a "three-chow/one-chow."

Consistently, I felt that rather than being paid to become the best copywriter I could be, I was being paid to improve my political skills. Finally after seven years of feasting on hefty expense-account dinners in glamourous clothes while having a famine of creativity, I decided I wanted out. I fantasized about becoming a *real writer* with free time—a profession where I could grow as a provocative, original thinker and communicator—my true passion.

Unfortunately, by the time I *truly* realized this, I was raking in big bucks—a six-figure income at age 27. How could I give this up? Or, I guess the real question was:

Do you pick a job for its
cash-in value—or its passion value?

I went for the passion. Why? My "on-the-job research" as an ad exec had revealed to me that money does *not* bring happiness. So, I decided to quit and research how happiness can bring money. My research proved positive. Pursuing my passions proved profitable on many levels—and it has proven so for many of my friends, as well. I believe this is for two reasons.

1. When you do what you love, this is most likely where your true talent lies, so you'll stand out in your field.
2. You'll be so enthusiastic about your pursuit, you'll have more energy to jump over annoying obstacles in your path.

For example, look at these people:

Gill started off as a lawyer—but was bored. He always dreamed of making movies. So, at age 29, he left his law practice to work as a groveling, unpaid intern at a film-production company. He is now a highly successful film producer who recently garnered three awards at Sundance—and is gearing up to produce two more films.

Phyllis started off as a top commercial director's agent—but wanted to do something creative instead of just representing creative people. She left her job to start Leibowitz NYC, a stylish, successful, home-products company that specializes in products created from unusual textiles imported from India.

Stuart started off as an account exec in advertising, then decided he wanted to work full-time in a more visual business. He became friends with clients he serviced at L'Oreal, and they helped him switch over to the client side, as a marketing director of new product images.

Susan started off in public relations, then went through a "mid-wife crisis." She realized she wanted to be a midwife. She went to nursing school, and now delivers babies—instead of headlines—for a living.

All these people originally landed in the wrong career destination, then moved on, and are happier for it.

You Must Resist Job-in-the-Hand Jobs

Right now you may think it's easier to stay where you are, rather than seek new opportunities. "Things aren't *that* bad," you rationalize—maybe you *will* get a promotion next month—that same promotion promised two years back. I know, I know. It's exhausting even *thinking* about getting back on that career subway and going to a new company or even a new wing of your present company. Plus, you may wonder: Will you *ever* be able to make sense of those map squigglies? But you must stay determined.

The Purpose of Your Life Is to Find the Purpose of Your Life

There are no extra humans on this planet. You are here to do something. Some of us are meant to be doctors, others musicians, and at least one of us was put here to invent that plastic doohickey that holds up the pizza box. It's up to you to figure out your career destination and how to get there.

The problem is: Too many of us consult the wrong map.

Some of us wind up looking at an outdated map that doesn't show how old destinations have been closed down or how new, exciting destinations have been added. We're still heading toward some dream place that we picked back in college or grad school—maybe even *grade* school—and look how much we've changed in the meantime. Or we consult the map our parents gave us—or our friends gave us—or the media gave us. Basically, many of our career maps are the equivalent of the maps Columbus was given: wrong.

You Need to Find a Workable Map—and Sometimes This Means Creating Your Own Map—Following the Map of Your Inner Psyche

You know what I mean? If not—or even if so—or if you've just plain ol' had enough of those damn map analogies (I sure have) here's another way of putting it:

To get where you need to go, you must first see who you really are. Before you can do, you must be.

Now, to help whip into you the extreme importance of remembering the above, here's a good symbolic fable:

Which Came First: The Eagle or the Egg?

A little boy was wandering in the forest and came upon an eagle's nest. He plucked an egg, brought it back to his farm, and, giggling to himself, slid it under a mama-to-be chicken. Soon after, this chicken's eggs hatched, and there among the chicklets was a female eaglet. This little eaglet grew up with her chicken peers, learning all sorts of chicken habits: how to walk like a chicken, squawk like a chicken, eat like a chicken. This eagle did it all. However, no matter how passionately she put her all into her chicken existence, she always felt something was missing. She didn't know what, but she felt an inner emptiness. She tried to ignore it. Then one day she looked up in the sky and saw a beautiful bird, soaring freely among the clouds. She felt a pang of awe mixed with a weird sense of connection. She longed to be up there flying, too. But she wondered what her chicken pals would think. Then suddenly she thought: What the hell. She flapped her wings vigorously, and to her surprise, she took off into the air. That's when she realized that all along there was more to her than mere chickenhood. She was meant to fly—as well as cash in on some other pretty nifty eagle perks.

This fable brings me once again to this book's central theme—which I will quickly and dramatically repeat in the following beautifully bold italicized typeface:

THIS BOOK'S CENTRAL THEME:

Mastering your outer world means you must first master your inner world.

When you change your beliefs, you change your life. An eagle who still thinks it's a chicken won't be able to fly. You must know in your heart that YOU ARE AN EAGLE. This means not being afraid of being an eagle—not being afraid of what your chicken friends will think about your being an eagle—and not being afraid to leave your chicken life behind. Meaning: *You must unshackle your limited beliefs of who you are and dare to be who you really, really are so you can do what you are really, really meant to do.*

Today's Fantasy Role-Playing Exercises (and Tips for Cracking Whips)

A "Sixual" Release: Six Questions to Help You Discover What Turns You On

1. What do you fantasize about doing when/if you ever grow up?

List four fantasy careers in your journal. Keep in mind what John Stuart Mill said: "Every great movement must experience three stages: ridicule, discussion, adoption." While you are writing your list, these stages will probably go on internally—you'll think: *But* I'm too old to be an actress. *But* it's too competitive to be a screenwriter. *But* I'm not organized enough to have my own company. *But* companies like that don't like to hire women. You must command your negative mind to stop with the ridicule already, and start discussing and adopting. You can begin by operating under the *You Never Know Principle.* For instance, did Rocky go into the fight saying, "Hey I might not win"? Or did Sylvestor Stallone go into the movie business saying, "I'm just some chump. What do I know about film?"

2. What kind of character are you?

Which qualities and traits do you value? For example: Optimism. Guts. Peacefulness. Creativity. Logic. Honesty. Kindness. Toughness. Stability. Excitement. Variety. Consistency. Solitude. Enthusiasm. Openness. Confidence. Love of Travel. Altruism. Patience. Youthfulness. Stylishness. Sophistication. Wisdom. Knowledge.

3. What do you have to offer this world skill-wise?

It's important to concentrate on what you can give—not on whether there is an easy opening. Remember: Maintaining a Master Mentality will be a far more important determining factor in getting a job than any job statistics.

4. When you've lost track of time doing something, what is that something?

Your goal is to find a career where you can lose yourself— which is not to be confused with a career where you lose your self-esteem.

5. What is a fantasy day like?

What hours do you prefer? What environment do you want to live and work in? What clothes are you wearing on this day? How much time would you devote to social events versus personal time?

6. How do your four fantasy career goals in Question #1 compare to the answers you gave in Questions #2 through #5?

Visualize how each fantasy career goal would *truly* make you feel/be/do. *Ask yourself:* Which one fantasy career matches up most with who you want to feel like/be like/spend time like? For now, this one fantasy career goal will become your long-term goal. Don't panic if you're not a gazillion percent convinced this is your fantasy career. As we proceed through the next 29 days, you will be reevaluating (and re-reevaluating) your career choice.

Excite Yourself with a Mental Rental

*A*s Principle #7 states, your long-term goal must play the *dominant role* in your career. So, before you go to sleep tonight, rent a fantasy movie of your new career life. Close your eyes, and envision your career goal attained. Envision the amazing things you would feel like/have around you/be like. Envision the people you value in your life congratulating you. Write yourself a speech of what you would say when you told them about your achievement. Remember: *Believe and receive*—and the more you can believe, the more (and the quicker) you'll receive. It's like this: If you believe a building exists, then even if you get lost on your way to trying to find it, you'll keep driving because you know it exists. And you know what you're looking for. You must commit to staying disciplined in your search for your fantasy career. And remember: Most people don't know where they are going. You now have one up on them by picking a career destination.

Master Bait-ing

*J*im Carrey used what I call a *Master Bait Technique.* He wrote himself a check for $10 million and used this check as motivational bait to keep on plugging. I feel this particular Master Bait worked particularly well because Jim wrote the check for such a humongous amount. If he had tried to bait himself with, say, only $2 million—enough to pay a few months' rent—he might not have whipped himself into enough peak excitement to whip his competition's tushes. Ironically it can be easier to reach higher career goals than lower ones, because your excitement level is so much higher. So don't restrain yourself. Create your own Master Bait—and be sure to crack that whip at big offerings.

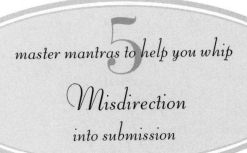

master mantras to help you whip **Misdirection** *into submission*

Whenever you are feeling a sense of wimpiness about staying true to your true career destination, remember:

1. I am not a SLAVE who says: "I don't have time to look at this #$@%! career map." I am a MASTER who knows how to make my career say: "Yes, master, whatever you say, master."

2. I am not a SLAVE who sees myself as a leaf in the wind. I am a MASTER who sees myself clearly and has a belief that I will win.

3. I am not a SLAVE who performs acts to please other peoples' career fantasies. I am a MASTER who acts out my hottest career fantasies in 3D Sensorama.

4. I am not a SLAVE who faces circumstances down on my knees afraid to move. I am a MASTER who fights circumstances by standing on my own two feet—and hightailing it back on that career subway.

5. I am not a SLAVE who is dominated by doubts and fears. I am a MASTER who lets my long-term career goal *dominate* my mind.

Whip

Fear

Into Submission

or

....

How to Be an Over-Fright Success Story

....

I was like the girl who cried wolf when it came to crying on—
and on—to friends about how I was going to quit my high-
paying/high-stressing/low–free time Sr. VP ad gig to pursue
a zero-paying wisp of a fantasy to be a writer. For nine
months, I kept saying it, but I was too afraid. Not just about
money. I also recognized that by not actually quitting I could
hold tightly on to a lovely fantasy about a parallel universe in
which I existed as "Happy-Go-Lucky Author Girl." I wasn't sure
if I wanted to risk giving up this fantasy.

Paradoxically, the more afraid I became to quit my job, the
less afraid I became of everything and everyone *at my job*. I kept
thinking: "So, what are they gonna do? Fire me?" That would
be job euthanasia. "Go ahead," I kept thinking. "Pull that plug.
Put me out of my misery." For example:

$\mathcal{I}$ tried a little
$\mathcal{S}$ & $\mathcal{M}$mmmmmmm.

For months my boss had been forcing me to write this goofy client-pleasing Motrin IB commercial that included one of those stereotypical mom/daughter aspirin-exchange-rite-of-passage scenarios. When the time came to read the storyboard, I ad-libbed a "hmmm" into the *script*—as in the mom saying "Motrin IB? Hmmm" to the daughter. The client enthusiastically commented how they *totally love-love-loved* this ad-libbed "hmmm" addition—could I *please* add it to the storyboard. I, nauseated by their disproportionate delight in a mere "hmmm" could not restrain myself from asking: "Do you want that to be a three-m 'hmmm' or a two-m 'hmm." Then I offered: "If you like—if you have flavored capsules—I could even make the mom say, 'Motrin IB, mmmmm.' "

Ironically, rather than being fired for the riskier things I said/wrote/did—I just kept getting raises. There is an old expression: "No money, half is gone. No courage, all is gone." Let me add: "Lots of courage, all is yours."

Fellow dominatrix Helen Keller had the right perspective on fear when she said: "Avoiding danger is no safer in the long run than outright exposure. The fearful are caught as often as the bold." You too must develop this Keller Attitude toward fear—and recognize that fear works like "inter-fear." It is the number one restraining choke collar that stops you from getting raises, getting a promotion, writing a riskier report, speaking up with a brilliant point at a meeting. Fearful people give off what I call:

$\mathcal{F}$earemones.

Everyone—bosses, employees, colleagues—can smell the fear on you, lessening your power. Consistently, fear is what *limits* you from getting the very best stuff in your career—and/or in fictional symbolic fables like the following:

Dope on a Rope

This criminal had committed a crime (because, hey, that's what criminals do). Anyway, he was sent to the king for his punishment. The king told him he had a choice. He could be hanged by a rope or take the punishment behind the big, dark, scary steel door. The criminal quickly decided on the rope. As the noose was being slipped on him, he asked: "Out of curiosity, what's behind that door?" The king laughed and said: "You know, it's funny, I offer all you guys the same choice, and nearly all of you pick the rope." "So," said the criminal, "what's behind the door? Obviously, I won't tell anyone," he said, pointing to the noose around his neck. The king paused, then answered, "Freedom, but it seems most people are so afraid of the unknown that they immediately take the rope."

Basically, we're all afraid of three things. Anything

1. New.
2. More.
3. Different.

Unfortunately for the faint of heart, moving forward in your career is all about the pursuit of new, more, different. Usually it's not until we find ourselves *dangling at the end of our rope* that we are motivated to triumph over this triumvirate. For instance:

After Sarah's boss wanted to rip her off for a huge commission, she finally had the courage to quit and pursue her own computer business.

After Greg's boss wanted to rip his clothes off, he finally had the courage to quit and pursue his own entrepreneurial investment ventures.

After Mark's boss in the fashion design department where he slaved became RIP—in other words, DEAD—and a new evil boss replaced her, he decided to put more effort into switching over to becoming a garment buyer.

Fear Today, Gone Tomorrow

*U*nfortunately, the one and only way to master fear is to actually do the thing you are most afraid of. Or as Chogyam Trungpa, author of *Shambala: The Sacred Path of The Warrior*, said: "True fearlessness is not the reduction of fear; but going beyond fear . . . by fear-less we don't mean 'less fear' but 'beyond fear.' "

How can you get to that beyond-fear place? Well, you know how it would be much easier for you to walk a plank that's on solid ground than one that's plunked over an alligator-infested lagoon, because the fear of all those yapping hungry alligators might make you less focused? In one's career, it's the same. As you know, there are always plenty of metaphorical yapping hungry alligators below you. The trick is: BE AWARE of them, but DON'T STARE at them. INSTEAD, DISCIPLINE YOURSELF TO STARE AT SOMETHING SAFE AND SOLID.

That's what I did. My courage to quit to become a writer finally came when I managed to stop staring at my alligators—which were plenty, including: *I'll never be published, being a writer is hyper competitive, what do I know about writing a book, what will I do for income—after all, I have a child to support—me.* Instead, I stayed focused on my supporting plank: my creative talents.

Some Dominate-trix

*G*ill, the award-winning film producer, tells himself before he goes into a meeting that everyone is more insecure than he is. It makes himself that much more confident.

Tangentially, another film producer says he always makes a point of firing someone at the beginning of each shoot, to put the fear in his staff to perform at peak levels. I'm not sure you want to follow this lesson—unless you're into creating a neurotic staff who are probably plotting a coup against you.

Today's Fantasy Role-Playing Exercises
(and Tips for Cracking Whips)

For Lasting Courage Try Listing Your Courage

*W*hat are you afraid of doing this afternoon at your job? Make a list of all your strengths that will help you beat your fears. Now make a list of examples from your past when you *DID* beat your fears. Next time you feel fear strike, strike back with these empowering lists. Remember: *High self-esteem is the opposite of fear. The more you trust yourself, the less you have to fear.*

Hire a Career Stunt Double

*W*ho scares you at your job? Wouldn't it be great if you had a stunt double to send in to deal with these people? Well, you do. Visualize a person whom you respect and believe to be courageous. Now imagine yourself as this person who marches into this intimidating person's office and convinces her to give you the special project you've had your eye on for the last month.

Master Stoke

*Y*ou can master your fears by stoking a larger fire of courage by finding a larger fear. For instance, alligators on a plank beneath you might be scary. But a tiger behind you is even scarier. Find that tiger.

My tiger was my co-op apartment.

After I bought it, I immediately had: *fear of mortgage payments.* I suddenly became aware that I was living a little beyond my means, and therefore had to work a little harder. No, a *lot* harder. Buying that apartment was sort of like buying a skirt that's a size too small as motivation to lose the weight. ANYWAY . . . I was at a party and met this guy, a successful MTV creative director. At first I was afraid to pitch myself as a freelancer. But my fear of mortgage payments helped me get over my fear of rejection.

A Painfully Direct Question Now That Will Direct You to Pleasure Later

*W*hat would you dare to dream to do if you knew you could not fail? How does this impact the long-term goal that you set for yourself on Day #1? For instance, let's say you wanted to look for the same job you have now—but in Paris? *Avez-vous la courage?*

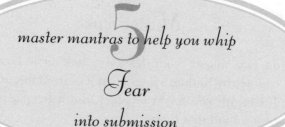

master mantras to help you whip

Fear

into submission

Whenever you feel your courage waning, remember:

1. I am not a SLAVE who is at the mercy of what comes to me. I am a MASTER who says *merci* to what I bring to myself.

2. I am not a SLAVE who thinks, "Not yet." I am a MASTER who thinks, "I get!"

3. I am not a SLAVE who fears a setback. I am a MASTER who sees failure as feedback.

4. I am not a SLAVE who talks to myself cruelly. I am a MASTER who talks to myself encouragingly.

5. I am not a SLAVE who restrains myself with limited thinking. I am a MASTER who retrains myself to see unlimited opportunity.

Whip

Cynicism

Into Submission

or

....

When You Climb the Corporate Ladder,
Be Sure You're Facing Upward, Not Downward

....

A lot of my friends think I'm one of the most positive people they know.

And I am positive.

Then again, I'm pretty damn cynical, too.

I've joked that a more realistic name for me might be "Karens" because there are definitely these two Karens (at least) living inside me. We here at Karen, Inc., are always trying to beat cynicism instead of allowing cynicism to beat us. Our strategy: Become a master interpreter of all ego-mangling, spirit-sapping circumstances. I always try to recognize:

*If at first you don't succeed
you're doing something stupid.*

When I graduated college, I interviewed at 23 ad agencies, and was told, oh, about 23 times, that the *only* way to get in the ad biz door was as a secretary. Being the impatient career gal that I am, I did not want to do time as a secretary. I wanted to get right into the trenches and create multimillion-dollar ads right away. So instead of interpreting each of those 23 failed interviews as taking me closer toward secretaryhood, I interpreted them as 23 steps toward learning how to become a better copywriter.

At each interview, I would *listen 110 percent actively* to my rejector's critique of my portfolio, then change it accordingly. One time I even ran to an arts supply store between interviews, and wrote and designed a brand-new campaign inspired by the previous interviewer's rejection. In the end, I not only got a copywriting gig at J. Walter Thompson, but my creative director asked me to show my portfolio to future interviewees, because he thought it was the best he'd ever seen.

The World Doesn't Suck If You Can Learn to Suck What You Can Out of the World

*Y*ou think 60,000 thoughts a day. Your goal is to make sure 59,999 of them are not cynical. Cynical thoughts drain energy and inspire negative behavior. As Henry Ford said: "If you think you can do a thing or if you think you can't, either way you are right." Your goal: *Change your thinking, one thought at a time until eventually you're able to work your way up to having all 60,000 out of 60,000 of your daily thoughts be positive.*

Remember: You alone determine what you think. You developed your present thinking pattern out of continual habit. Like all habits, you can change it with DISCIPLINE. Starting today you must train your mind to see unlimited possibilities where right now you see limitations. We here at Karen, Inc., know how hard this can be. But you must keep the faith—even when your faith gets out of breath.

A Very Surreal, Very True Story About Faith

J was walking down the street and saw this man standing by his car's steaming engine. Suddenly he looked up at me and yelled: "Faith! Faith! Where are you, faith?"

Then I heard this whiny, out-of-breath female voice behind me. "Relax, I'm coming!"

I turned and saw this short, plump, middle-aged woman running toward him: Faith.

I had to laugh. This was not what I imagined Faith to look like—though it does fit Faith's description: oft times lagging, but there when you need it.

You Must Practice Faith Daily and Nightly, and In-Betweenly

W hen you start having faith in miracles, you start seeing miracles. Which reminds me of an old joke.

H_2-Uh-Oh

A man was drowning in the ocean, hoping maybe God might save him. Soon a small boat rowed up and offered to help him, but he, still testing to see if God would save him, sent the boat away. Next a big yacht came by and offered to help him, but he sent this yacht away, again testing to see if God would save him. Next a helicopter flew by and offered to throw down a ladder, but the man sent the helicopter away, still holding out for God to save him. Soon after, he drowned. When this man got up to heaven, he asked God why he didn't save him. God explained: "Who do you think sent the boat, the yacht, the helicopter?"

You're being sent boats, yachts, helicopters all the time. They may not look like what you imagined, but you just have to JUMP ON BOARD.

For instance:

I have a writer friend who is a practicing Buddhist. Every morning he wakes up and chants for money—sometimes for up to two hours. ANYWAY . . . he's been sending out his screenplay, to no avail. I offered to help. When he showed it to me, I immediately saw his format was not what film companies consider professional. I explained how if a film executive sees a nonstandard format, he'll assume its a substandard script and won't even bother to read it. But my friend refused to change the format, explaining it would take too much time.

P.S. He still hasn't sold it—though, paradoxically, his chanting DID work. I was his God-sent helicopter. I was sent to him to explain how to make money, but he didn't take the helicopter ride.

P.P.S. Faith can move mountains, but not paperwork. You must put in a little effort behind your faith.

Blind Faith

Scott's career as a TV producer was careening along full force when, out of nowhere, he developed a vision problem. He was told in time he'd become legally blind. He approached his boss and told him, "This is incurable. Apparently I can't do anything: drive, read, cross the street. I have no clue as to how I'm going to work in TV." He left it there, expecting his boss to let him go. Instead his boss responded: "Scott, you have a lot of problems. You are lazy, disorganized, irresponsible. You have a lot of things to work on. Go back and work on those things. If you have trouble with your eyesight, let me know." Scott was overwhelmed by his boss' generosity of faith. He decided to take on the challenge, and prove to his boss that he made the right decision.

Get a Fire in Your Belly—Not an Ulcer

*S*cott's boss obviously made the right choice, because Scott has since worked his butt off and become a senior vice president at Nickelodeon. His secret? "I've come to grips with my loss of vision, mourned it," explains Scott. "I understand who I am. I love myself as imperfect person. What drives me is the love I have for making things—cool, creative things I'm proud of. It's important to me not to be patronized for my work. I never want people to say: 'Nice work for a blind guy.' "

Today's Fantasy Role-Playing Exercises
(and Tips for Cracking Whips)

Is There a Spin Doctor in the House?

*W*hat ego-mangling, spirit-sapping circumstances are making you feel cynical now? Pretend these are somebody else's problems and you are a Master Spin Doctor for his career. (After all, it's much easier to see the silver lining in *someone else's* cloud.) How would you convince this other person that the bad things happening are actually good things? Now let these positive interpretations dominate over your cynicism.

Swallow a Cocktytale

*N*ext time you're about ready to give up on a project, a job opportunity, a report—or if you've simply been walking around thinking JUST SHOOT ME NOW—*pour yourself a cockytale*. Tell yourself one tale that makes you cocky. Recall a time you blew away a room with your presentation. Or think about someone who got the kind of job you have your eye on— *and you know you're blessed with more talent than he is. You'll get it—easily. Make yourself swagger.* Next, tell yourself that your present negative situation is merely temporary. Repeat aloud: "I CHOOSE FAITH." Do it now. Even if you feel this sounds like a lie, go ahead, lie to yourself. Heck, everyone else is lying to you, so why not join the crowd?

Believing Is Seeing

*D*ecide today to believe that there is a bright side to every negative work assignment and/or person you meet. Eventually you can train yourself to see life more positively. It's sort of like that time I painted my living room this beautiful marbleized yellow. (Actually I *pointed*. Someone else *painted*.) ANYWAY . . . after that, because it was inputted into my brain, I started noticing marbleized painted walls in places I'd never noticed them before—like in the bathroom of the Space Untitled Cafe where I do my writing.

The same new vision quest has happened with my work life, too. One summer my friends were all planning a time-share in the Hamptons. I wanted to join in on the fun, but I also wanted to save my nest egg money from my Miramax deal—so I wouldn't later wind up with nest egg on my face, you know? I was starting to feel cynical about ever earning the extra income. ANYWAY . . . I was over at Miramax and they were telling me how much they loved the titles I gave my books (e.g., my novel

50% Off, plus *How to Make Your Man Behave in 21 Days or Less Using the Secrets of Professional Dog Trainers,* plus *How To Succeed in Business Without a Penis).* Meryl, my development person, joked I should retitle their movies. The next thing I knew I was doing it for real. Afterward, like a miracle, I suddenly could see how this could be a great cash-in opportunity with other film and TV companies I knew.

Let's Make a Deal

*M*ake a deal with yourself to only be cynical during a certain time of day for five minutes. Take one cynical break a day.

Go to Bed with a Group of Fun People

*T*onight before you go to sleep, list the people in your life who have positive attitudes. Vow to spend more time with them.

A Painfully Direct Question Now That Will Direct You to Pleasure Later

*H*ow does your cynicism impact your long-term goal? For instance, let's say you stopped thinking it's *impossible* to become a senior vice president at your age or stage.

master mantras to help you whip

5

Cynicism

into submission

Next time you feel cynicism sinking in, remember:

1. I am not a SLAVE who sees conflicts. I am a MASTER who sees lessons.

2. I am not a SLAVE who sees endings. I am a MASTER who sees beginnings.

3. I am not a SLAVE who sees grapes of wrath. I am a MASTER who sees *raisons d'êtres.*

4. I am not a SLAVE who sees problems as stumbling blocks. I am a MASTER who sees problems as stepping stones.

5. I am not a SLAVE who chants for success—but doesn't act. I am a MASTER who leaps on a chance—and acts.

Whip

Regret

Into Submission

or

Living in the Past Is Like Driving Forward
While Looking in the Rearview Mirror

I often feel like I am an honorary member of the WHAT WAS I THINKING CAREER CLUB. I was an especially active member a few years ago when I was bicoastal, taking meetings in L.A. to host my own television show. At one point I was simultaneously offered a development deal with a production company and an on-air opportunity with a cable TV network. When it came time to play Let's Make a TV Deal, I took what was behind the production company's door of opportunity—foolishly turning down the cable TV network *before I got this other offer firmly in writing.*

To quote Forrest Gump: "Stupid is as stupid does."

Whenever I think about how this production company manipulated me, I can work myself into a Tourette's syndrome state of mind. I want to start barking—or better yet biting. I find myself obsessing over the past: They did this, she said that, he made me think yet another thing. So I try not to think about it, knowing:

Regret is pain relived instead of pain relieved.

When it comes to regret, you must discipline yourself to follow the opposite of that Nike slogan:

Just don't do it.

Learn your lesson, then move on. Just look at where looking backward got Lot's wife. You know what I'd like to see? A new strain of Alzheimer's that conveniently rids its victims strictly of disturbing memories. Were you fired? Rejected? Humiliated? Did you foolishly not get an L.A. producer's offer in writing before turning down another offer? Don't fret—forget.

However, before you forget, you must ALSO remember:

You must turn all bad experiences into "inperiences."

You must fully take into your mind, into your spirit, into your cells *what you learned*—then vow to avoid making these mistakes in the future. For instance, before I moved onward from my wayward LA experience, I took in the following lessons:

1. Get it in writing.
2. Everybody lies. Trust no one.
3. No more Ms. Nice Guy.
4. Inside every bad job experience is a great job opportunity just waiting to burst forth.

Transform Regret Into Get, Get, Get

I eventually enjoyed the rewards of Lesson #4 by transform-ing my failed TV deal into a valuable book deal. Soon af-ter LA proved to be spelled more like LIE, I gobbled up every business book in sight. I read *The Art of War, The Prince, What They Don't Teach You in Harvard Business School*—etc, etc. I scheduled lunches with older professionals who I felt could help me develop new insights about my career. Then I took what I learned and channeled it into my *How To Succeed in Business Without a Penis* book—which went on to become a national bestseller.

In Japan, the Word for "Crisis" Also Means "Opportunity"

S imilarly, in the Land of Karen, the word "experience" also means "boy was I an idiot." Just kidding. Seriously, I al-ways try NOT to focus on regrets, but instead on the lessons I get. This applies not only to large regrets, but to small ones, too. For instance: "Why did I say that? Why *didn't* I say that? Why did I do that? Why *didn't* I do that? Why did I/*didn't* I: wear that, eat that, buy that, *date* that???"

Basically, all regrets are lucky breaks in disguise—the prob-lem is, some of these disguises are of the scary werewolf-mask variety. But, no matter. You must remind yourself not to respond with a Slave Mentality to regret by kicking yourself repeatedly, and instead use your regrets to kick bad habits.

46

From Gold Mine to Gold Yours to Gold Mind

apoleon Hill, author of *Think and Grow Rich*, offers an inspiring story about regret turning into get, get, get. Hill writes
about a businessman who bought a plot of land and gold-drilling
machinery. After drilling for years, without any sign of a buried
treasure, he sold his land and equipment to a junk man—who dug
a mere three feet deeper and found a treasure trove of gold.

In a word: ouch.

This businessman could have slunk into a downward spiral
of regret. Instead, thereafter, every time he was ready to give up
on a business opportunity, he'd repeat his own tailor-made
mantra: JUST THREE MORE FEET TO GO, JUST THREE
MORE FEET TO GO.

He eventually made his millions in a variety of future busi-
nesses.

And then there's that guy who made pennies . . . Abraham
Lincoln.

Lincoln's Thinkin'

incoln, at age 22, was defeated in a legislative race. At age
26, his sweetheart died. At age 27, he had a nervous
breakdown. At age 34, he lost a congressional race. At age 36,
he lost again. At age 45, he lost a senatorial race. At age 47, he
lost as vice president. At age 49, he lost another senatorial race.
Then, finally, at age 52, Lincoln—because of his ability not to
focus on the past, but to stay focused on his future—FINALLY
became President of the United States. His secret? He knew:

You must make your past a thing of the future.

Doug, president of Crunch, a popular health club chain, also
cashes in on Lincoln's thinkin'. Doug is always telling himself

that if he misses out on an opportunity, it's because there's something better waiting in his future. For instance, one time he missed out on jumping on a good deal for computer equipment. Seven months later, the technology leaped light-years ahead, so the computer equipment he ultimately bought made him look like a genius for waiting.

You—like Doug—must also maintain an abundance mentality about regrets—and that does not mean thinking that there's an abundance of bad experiences waiting to happen. It means unshackling limited thinking, and recognizing unlimited opportunities.

Today's Fantasy Role-Playing Exercises
(and Tips for Cracking Whips)

Find the Meaning in Life's Meanness

What are some business regrets you've had in the last five years? The last year? The last month? Today? Now look at your regrets and write a second list beside each regret of the lessons you learned. Turn all your bad experiences into "inperiences," and let these lessons DOMINATE your mind instead of your lessened hope. Remember: You can only hold one thought at a time. It's your pick of which thought to hold in your mind:

1. Life sucks.
2. I can suck the good stuff out of life.
3. Or (my personal favorite) George Clooney lying naked on a bearskin rug.

Which Branch of the What Was I Thinking Club Are You Eligible For?

*L*ook at the list of regrets that you wrote. What do you have more of: "Why didn't I?" or "Why did I?" Depending on your answer, you now know that you need to work more on being either more cautious or more spontaneous.

Register for a Master Card

*W*rite the following on a card: "No single job opportunity has a future. ONLY I—and I alone—have a future." Whenever regrets sneak up on you, sneak a peek at this card. Remember: A bad end to a job or a project is not the end of a career—it is the beginning of something new. Nature abhors a vacuum—almost as much as I abhor to vacuum.

Create a Master Peace

*T*hink about your one biggest, most painful regret. Now create your own tailor-made mantra—like that gold-digging businessman—that you can use to make peace with it.

A Painfully Direct Question Now That Will Direct You to Pleasure Later

*H*ow does your long-term goal from yesterday change when you remove your regret from yesteryear? For example, what would happen if you stopped regretting that you put in all those years at law school, let go, and allowed yourself to leave law to open up your own restaurant?

master mantras to help you whip

Regret

into submission

Next time you feel yourself regressing into regret, remember:

1. I am not a SLAVE who sees problems as stumbling blocks. I am a MASTER who sees problems as stepping stones.

2. I am not a SLAVE who lets myself be beaten down by failure. I am a MASTER who becomes a person based upon who I choose to be.

3. I am not a SLAVE who sees a setback. I am a MASTER who sees a way to get back.

4. I am not a SLAVE who sees obstruction. I am a MASTER who sees instruction.

5. I am not a SLAVE who asks: "Why me?" I am a MASTER who asks: "What next?"

Whip

Anger

Into Submission

or

....

Behind Every Successful Woman
Is Someone Who Pissed Her Off

....

I'm mad at me. I've even stopped talking to me. And I won't even have sex with me. Though actually I'm not *really* mad at me. I'm really mad at Steve. (Note: Not his real name. His real name is Dinkhead.) ANYWAY . . . Steve told me he'd have dubs of my on-air video reel finished today—no questions asked.

Now I'm asking questions. For instance: Why the heck didn't I call Steve yesterday to remind him? Why do people call him Steve when his real name is Dinkhead? And if that's his real name, then are he and I related?

It's Better to Be Pissed Off Than Pissed On

I'm not alone in my knee-jerk-me-jerk self-blame reaction to anger. Many women take the anger they have for others and turn it inward. It's one of those male versus female/Mars versus Venus things. But self-anger is Slave Mentality. We must learn not to beat ourselves up every time something goes wrong. As my grandmother used to say:

"Once fucked over, shame on you. Twice fucked over, shame on me." (Only Grandma didn't say it quite like that. But I feel her sentiment holds.)

You Must Get Into Cross Training

*Y*ou must train yourself to get cross in the correct way. Through conscious thought you must choose to have a conscious response to anger, recognizing that rational communication begets rational communication—whereas bitchiness can be a boomerang.

In other words:

The wrong approach might mean your departure.

Speak too soon, and you could be fired very soon—or resented later. Although actions may speak *louder* than words, words speak *longer.* I've found a good way to deal with anger is to understand fully where your anger is coming from. Often when you are angry, *it's because you're being a slave to your past.* I believe many of us carry around with us what I call a PORTABLE CHILDHOOD. We set up our childhood dynamics wherever we may be, casting a colleague in the daddy role, or our boss in the mommy role—or all too often in the mommy dearest role. In other words, we reenact our childhood dramas with whomever we have handily around us. For instance, if a colleague is late to meet you, and you had a father who was always late to pick you up from ballet class, your colleague's tardiness could trigger an anger response that's stronger than he deserves. Hence, it's wise to apply the Buddhist approach to anger:

Respond, don't react.

You know how at the beach, it's smart to wait about an hour after eating before you go flouncing into the water? Well, the same goes for letting anger digest before you go jumping in. Count ten "fuck yous" before you speak your mind. Oh—and here's the hard part: You should count those "fuck yous" *silently to yourself.*

You Must Develop Mind Over Madder

Through conscious thought, you can become aware of *why* you are angry, and *what* you want to do with this anger. It's up to you. You can:

1. Foolishly let anger distract you from your goal—incorporating the Slave Mentality.
2. Wisely channel anger into positive energy that propels you more quickly to your goal—incorporating the Master Mentality.

Obviously I believe a Master Mentality beats the bupkiss out of slavehood. You'll find that when you become the master of your anger, you will even start to see anger as a welcome impetus to *not only say* you're going to achieve goals, *but help you be better committed to achieving them.* As I've joked to friends, "Sometimes you have to reach 'Fuck This!' to get to 'Post Fuck This'—which has always been my most action-packed, valuable career time."

My friend Christina agrees. She was working at a magazine for an editor who was—as Christina says—"a renowned bitch." Other assistants had problems with her, too. Christina longed to quit her job and put together a book idea she had called *The Smart Girl's Guide to College.* So Christina channeled her anger against her boss into writing a saleable book proposal—while keeping in mind:

You must never burn a bridge behind you— unless a raft is waiting.

Christina explains: "I became so miserable at my job that I just kept working harder and harder on my proposal. Finally I subconsciously—and I think somewhat consciously—put myself in a position to be fired, so I would be forced to do what I really wanted to do: publish my book."

It all worked out perfectly in the end. Christina left her job and got published—receiving highly favorable reviews for her book. Christina says, "If I hadn't been working for a woman who was a horrible human being, I'd be doing nothing much with my career. I have a much better career now—thanks to her."

As they say: Success is the best revenge. Though sometimes *revenge* can be the best revenge. (Just kidding, just kidding.)

Today's Fantasy Role-Playing Exercises
(and Tips for Cracking Whips)

Go on a No-Nuts Diet

Just like there's sexual attraction, there's hate attraction. If someone does something to you that pisses you off, your anger can grow stronger and stronger as you spend more and more time with this person—unless your anger is released. Forgiving someone is actually an act of self-interest. After all, you can't work at peak performance when your anger is focused on bringing someone else down. Your attention on the nut down the hall will wind up taking your attention off your wonderful talents and positive career opportunities. Some people think suffering aids creativity. Pshaw. I do my best work when peaceful inside. Hence, I try to live by the adage: Peace on earth for all mankind—except Steve. (Just kidding.) A good exercise to exorcise anger is to write a list of the people who drive you nuts, and vow to forgive them—then forget about them.

Burning Angry

The following is an ancient ritual believed to help release even the deepest wrath: Write down on a piece of paper three things that truly get your ire up. Now honestly ask yourself—are your three things tied up with your childhood? If so, acknowledge the anger connection—then attempt an anger rejection by setting your ire on fire. Burn your list. As you watch your hot temper turn into ashes before your eyes, tell yourself so does your anger.

What Are the Things That Make You Go Mmmfgruphn#$@*%?

What are the things that would piss you off if you didn't get your fantasy career? Use this list to feed the fire of your career desire when you find your passion dying down.

Try the Tri-Master

....

*N*ext time someone tries to screw you over, or lies to you, or spreads a vicious rumor about you, or doesn't keep a deadline—and you've done what needs to be done to deal with this goofball, but somehow your anger won't shift out of Mafiosa Revenge Mode—command your mind to remember the positives that are in it for you to move onward. Remind yourself that anger is self-inflicted pain. It is harmful to your body, mind, and spirit. Your goal is to create a dynamic triumvirate: COOL MIND, WARM HEART, HOT BODY. Study this Tri-Master over and over: COOL MIND, WARM HEART, HOT BODY. Remember: When your mind has a positive target to direct its energies toward, you'll bring more and more positive things to you. Of course this isn't easy. It requires the discipline of an athlete preparing for an event—this event being the rat race.

Surly to Bed, Surly to Rise

....

*T*onight decide you will not go to bed angry about *anything* that happened today.

master mantras 5 *to help you whip*

𝒜*nger*

into submission

Next time you feel an anger storm hovering, remember:

1. I am not a SLAVE who, when angry, winds up getting
pissed on. I am a MASTER who knows just how to get
pissed off.

2. I am not a SLAVE who has an unconscious reaction
to anger. I am a MASTER who responds with conscious
action to anger.

3. I am not a SLAVE who unconsciously accepts misery.
I am a MASTER who consciously chooses mastery

4. I am not a SLAVE who is controlled by the whims of
what people say. I am a MASTER who knows I have the
power to control what I hear.

5. I am not a SLAVE who makes myself a whipping post
for others. I am a MASTER who takes that career whip
in hand.

Whip

Worry

Into Submission

or

....

You're Not Being Paid to Freak Out

....

Speaking of incredible sex—well, even if we weren't, I'm sure you secretly want to. Anyway, incredible sex is all about being in the present moment, not getting caught up in worries. As soon as you start worrying if your thighs look fat in a particular position—or if that rustle in the other room is your husband home early from work—the passion starts crashing. Well . . .

58

Worry Can Make You Impotent
in Both the Bedroom and Boardroom Alike

*W*orry works like a magnet, attracting the very thing you're eager to avoid: anticlimactic performances. For instance, if I start to worry I won't be able to write this chapter on worry, then I will suddenly find myself writing *mfghy thyj jlungpluy mhuyt jhuklsh#$%@?* If you know what I mean.

Spiritual practioners recognize the self-fulfilling side effects of worry with two famous quotes:

Worry is a prayer for something you don't want.

And:

*Everything is created twice.
First in thought, then in reality.*

Spiritual practioners believe it's a good idea to keep conversations—even those that go on just in your pretty little head—consistent with what you want to happen, which is good advice for everyone, even those who don't have spiritual leanings. Even psychologists agree. They believe worry can psychologically play itself out as a self-fulfilling prophecy. Muhammad Ali cashed in on the psych-you-out effects of worry when he fought George Foreman. He recited chants meant to fill George with worries. It worked. Georgie crumbled.

A Hazardous Time Waste Material

*W*orry is one of the most wasted mental energies there can be—and one of the hardest habits to let go of. Especially for folks like me who have what I call a WAIT PROBLEM. I hate to wait to hear about the *results* of a manuscript or a presentation. I want to know everything NOW. I need to constantly remind myself that:

Worry must not be confused with preparation.

Only rarely can worry actually be used for preparation—as a stimulus to improve your work, or create a titillating sense of excitement in your life that makes you feel more joy. Unfortunately, worry is rarely used for these end benefits. Most of the time most of us worry about things *we can do nothing about*—what the client will think of the report that's already in FedEx airspace, what the boss is going to say during his "surprise" announcement this afternoon, whether a potential client will choose your services over those of competitors. Yet on some level we are foolishly convinced that all of this worry will magically influence our future.

Alan Watts, author of many Taoist books, including *The Wisdom of Insecurity*, said it well when he said: "Our lives are one long effort to resist the unknown." The "unknown" affects everyone and everything on this planet—right down to teeny weeny electrons. Even your local quantum physicist canNOT predict the future of PET laboratory electrons when they are let loose in experiments. Sometimes electrons live the life of a wave, sometimes of a particle—a quantum physicist never knows for sure. So, if *even* a smart quantum physicist can't predict the future of an electron—one of the teeniest particles found in this vast universe—then you are no better off trying to lay down bets on where that bigger and lumpier chunk of the universe called "Your Career" is going.

Slowing Up

*Y*ou know how when you're trying too hard to remember someone's name you never can? It's only when you let go, relax, stop being so anxious—stop *worrying*—that the name appears. The same goes for coming up with solutions for work problems that you're worried about. You must slow down during stressful times, practice "energy management." When you store up the energy you put into worry and channel it, you can get more work done. For this reason, slowing down can actually speed you up.

Action Heroes or Still Heroes?

*Y*ou know how in action movies Clint and Sigourney can remain cool and collected even when their futures look bleak and doomed? That's because they are masters of the art of staying still within. Although the characters these actors play are called *action heroes*, their real resonance and appeal comes from being *still heroes*—by remaining calm in stressful situations when most of us would be freaked out with fear. The Buddhists call this stillness "mindfulness." Though in many ways its like mind-*unfull*-ness, because it's about emptying your mind of expectations and worry.

For instance, Susan, a buyer at Macy's, recently taught herself the art of "slowing up." She was waiting for a shipment of winter clothes that seemed to be lost in transit. "I was getting all freaked out. Then I told myself 'Shhh.' I even said it out loud like that. Then I reminded myself that each five minutes of worrying I did were five minutes of work I *wasn't* doing that should be done, so I could avoid more problems that might then become more things to worry about."

Meditation can also help you "slow up," by enabling your mind to become more peaceful, so your subconscious can come up with the right answers. I credit writing the first draft of my screenplay for *50% Off* to meditating for a half an hour twice daily. At first glance, meditation sounds easy—doing nothing but lying there like a lump. But ironically doing nothing can be more difficult that doing too many somethings. (Perhaps because doing too many somethings can be yet another way of doing too little of what you really have to do.) However, time and time again I've found that meditation works like one of those shake-up snow-dome thingies. It helps the flaky stuff in your mind settle down, so you can see more clearly what's truly underneath.

Today's Fantasy Role-Playing Exercises
(and Tips for Cracking Whips)

Worry About Failure Holds You Back
More Than Actual Failure

*I*t's self-defeating living in a tense future tense. So next time you feel worried about performing in a presentation, or how you performed post-presentation, COMMAND your mind to focus on your long-term goal. Basically, the trick is to have great nonexpectations about which specific presentations/interviews/events will get you to your long-term goal, while maintaining a consistently positive attitude about *reaching your long-term goal*. Always remember: *No one presentation or report or interview will make you or break you.*

Meditation Can Work Like Medication

*O*nce a day, rest your hyper mind with a little meditation. Stop, sit, close your eyes. Become a human still life. Be nothing. Do nothing. Except breathe. Be at one with your breath. In and out, in and out. Shhh and ignore the shhhit.

Using Naughty Words

*B*an the following words from your vocabulary: "I'm worried that . . ." "What if . . ." "I should have said . . ." "I should never have said . . . !" "I'll have another scotch on the rocks."

Failure in Many Ways Is More Like Fullure

*W*hat could be the worst thing that could happen to you in your career? COMMAND your mind to recognize that worrying about this thing will not help or hinder—well, maybe hinder if you worry too much. Then COMMAND your mind to know that there is no such thing as you being a total loser even if this worst thing happens, either. Successful people all recognize that failure is always full of stuff you can learn and grow from. Remember: Every single person (your boss included) has felt like he has completely, utterly blown a presentation and/or experienced feeling like a helpless, nerve-wracked mess—and everyone has eventually seen how chock full of learning experience each and every failure has later proven to be.

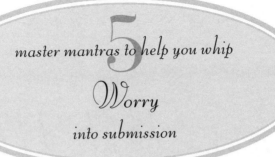

master mantras to help you whip

Worry

into submission

Next time you feel worry buzzing around you, remember:

1. I am not a SLAVE who tries to guess the future. I am a MASTER who knows I am here now . . . no, no, *now* . . . no, NOW.

2. I am not a SLAVE who worries about problems, failures, conflicts. I am a MASTER who says: "Tough beans what happens. I'm gonna do what I can do in this given time."

3. I am not a SLAVE who gets jumpy about what will happen. I am a MASTER who believes, "Jump and the net will appear."

4. I am not a SLAVE who wants guarantees. I am a MASTER who knows I can handle whatever comes upon me.

5. I am not a SLAVE who spends time being worried. I am a MASTER who spends more time just being in the moment.

Whip
Your Bad Mood
Into Submission

or

....

You Must Believe in a Laughter Life

....

I was taking a phone break—from writing this very book you're reading—talking with my pal Tessa, when suddenly I looked down at my computer and caught a lightning storm flash across its screen. In a word: yikes. I was hoping it was temporary bad weather conditions, and would soon pass. It didn't. So I rushed the computer to the repair shop, where the guy looked at it, then gave his autopsy: "Dead."

"Okay, Comedy Girl," I told myself, "Yeah, you with the funny books. Find the humor in this one."

I did.

"So my *data* is now *deada*," I said. "And I guess now I'm going to be in *debta* because I'm gonna have to buy a whole new *computa*."

Humor Is the Best Medicine—
the Original Prozac

*I*t's literally good medicine to laugh. Many doctors even prescribe renting funny movie videos to patients, recognizing the restorative benefits of hooting it up. Physiologically it goes like this: A smile sets off a stream of happy endorphins throughout your body, like a Rube Goldberg toy. When you flex the facial muscles necessary to smile, you decrease the flow of blood to nearby vessels, which cools the peripheral blood, which lowers the temperature of blood to the brain stem, which then produces less of a neurostransmitter called serotonin, which then puts you in a perkier mood. Plus, biologists have also documented how persons who are happy are better able to retrieve happy thoughts/ideas from their brains, because these information bits simmer at similar temperatures. So:

Just as the rich get richer, the happy get happier.

It's hard, I know, to maintain a happy disposition—that is, if you're over four years old. It seems the under-five-years-old segment of the population has a far easier time laughing at just about anything. Food drops on the floor—it's funny. Mom can't find her car keys—hilarious. Researchers have documented how the average four-year-old laughs about 500 times a day. Unfortunately, we adults are lucky if we get in ten laughs a day—and luckier still if those laughs are during the workday.

Take my neighbor Paul Down the Hall. He says this about his career life: "Only about 1 percent of this country are happy with their career, and they just *think* they are. They just don't know they're really miserable."

Many of us have an Inner Paul living inside us. I used to. I used to be very suspicious of people who were too happy with their careers, believed them to have dead people parts in their freezer. Then I realized the secret to happiness:

Happiness is not about what happens to you, but how you choose to respond to what happens.

A good dominatrix of one's destiny always keeps this perspective in mind, and makes it a dominant priority to develop an uncanny ability to be a master interpreter of all problems—to seek the pleasure in all her pain, aware that pain is a good teacher. She knows that life is more than this present moment, and that: COMEDY = TRAGEDY + 3 MONTHS + 4 MARGARITAS. Or to quote the philosopher Arthur Schopenhauer:

"Life may be compared to a piece of embroidery of which, during the first half of our time, we get a sight of the right side, and during the second half, of the wrong. The wrong side is not as pretty . . . but it is more instructive; it shows the way in which the threads have been worked together [to make the pattern]."

This Arty guy has definitely got the right Master Mentality.

Job slaves, on the other hand, fail to see the humor in all the bad things that invariably happen at an office. They defeatedly and overseriously accept the yucky stuff around them—and are thereby unable to see past it to an unyucky future.

The Funny Anecdote Antidote

*E*very time something goes wrong, I now purposefully call a friend and consciously try to tell this unfunny painful situation as a funny anecdote—or hope that my friend can help me find the humor in it. For example, when I was working in advertising, together a friend and I renamed this guy Harry—this spineless boss I had—as "THE WORM." We even came up with a series of expressions for him: "THAT WILL OPEN UP A CAN OF HARRYS." And: "THE EARLY BIRD CATCHES THE HARRY." This nicknaming helped me deal with my boss in all future spineless scenarios. I've also found that after indulging in an Anecdote Antidote, I'm better able to see an answer to the very unfathomable situation I've just complained about.

You know that expression: "It only hurts when I laugh"? For me it works the other way around. It's when I *don't* see something as funny that I feel the pain.

Consistently, humor is a miraculous enlightening agent, because it lessens your stress, and thereby frees up energy for problem solving. Plus, as I noted earlier, biologists have researched how the brains of happy, peppy, positive people are better able to retrieve happy, peppy, positive ideas. This is why I recommend that:

You must crack that whip at cracking yourself up.

Consider some of the advice of the following crack-up addicts:

Kera, a book editor, has two phone numbers she and her office mates call to hoot it up when things get bad: the Time Warner Lady, a Spock-meets-Deepak-Chopra inspirational recording, and the Lunch Lady, a "very David Letterman" kitschy kitchen listing.

Julie, a senior VP at Nickelodeon, looks for a good sense of humor in all the people she hires. Plus she surrounds herself with toys to play with, to put herself into jovial spirits during a stressful day.

Laura, a lawyer, has a Virex program on her computer that offers a laugh track called "Hysterical" that just laughs nonstop. Whenever she's bummed, she plays this hysterical laughter and finds it to be contagious.

Thomas Edison, inventor of the light bulb, understood the importance of humor to success. He failed 10,000 times before he came up with a workable light bulb. When asked his secret to success he joked: "I failed so many times that the only thing left to do was to succeed—I exhausted all the failures."

Today's Fantasy Role-Playing Exercises
(and Tips for Cracking Whips)

Political Incorrections

*W*henever I know I'm going to appear on the TV show *Politically Incorrect,* I start reading the newspaper with a different perspective. I purposefully assign myself to look for the funny angles in all current events. For example, I noticed how every time there's a horrific murder, Hollywood gets a hell-of-a-woody, seeing it as a money-making movie. So I joked that criminals, rapists, and murderers should start going to Hollywood producers to pitch their crimes beforehand to see if there's a movie deal in the works for them. Today as you read each news article, view it with a funny perspective. Relate two unrelated events—or seek out the paradoxical, the ironic, the lighthearted splash of optimism in the wave of bad news. I recommend this as a regular exercise to keep your brain in upbeat working order.

Before and Laughter

*A*sk yourself how your favorite comedian would describe a work situation that is making you miserable. See life through Woody Allen's glasses. Or Roseanne's contact lenses.

Cryogenics

*Y*ou should never cry at the office. So if by chance you feel yourself on the verge of hysterical tears, freeze your crying before it reaches Tammy Faye Bakker, runny-mascara level, and remind yourself that when you thaw out your problem later that night, you will find the humor in it—*somewhere*. Decide right now that you—as a master of your destiny—will always try to find a way to laugh hysterically instead of simply getting hysterical.

Funny Business

Next time you want to encourage yourself to get back into a funny frame of mind: Read a funny book. Rent a funny video. Seek out a funny friend. Or seek out a wise dead person, like William Shakespeare, who said: "There is nothing either good or bad, but thinking makes it so."

Mood Food

Sugar is a recognized chemical downer. Whenever you feel your mood heading south, try to stay clear from cookies, candy, cake—even fruit juices. Oh . . . and here's another good recipe for laughter. Make a lunch date today with someone you know who is successful and funny and happy (and Prozac-free.)

Turn Your Blues Into Green

Next time you feel like the world's biggest goofball, kick this goofball habit out of vision by reminding yourself how your present accomplishments were once fucked-up situations, too. Command your mind to remember: YOU LIVE AND LEARN—and better yet: YOU LIVE AND EARN! And even better yet: YOU LIVE AND SHOP.

Next time you think Kevorkian has the right approach to pain, remember:

1. I am not a SLAVE who says: "What's so funny?" I am a MASTER who says: "A funny thing happened to me on the way to my promotion."

2. I am not a SLAVE who only sees the serious side to business. I am a MASTER who is able to enjoy a little funny business.

3. I am not a SLAVE who has a breakdown over work problems. I am a MASTER who cracks up over work problems.

4. I am not a SLAVE who only sees the dark side to problems. I am a MASTER who knows a light is shining on the other side.

5. I am not a SLAVE who thinks God is a sadist. I am a MASTER who knows God is a jokester.

Whip

Blame

Into Submission

or

....

I'm Okay, Everybody Else Sucks

....

"If only my agent hadn't died," said Pam, "I'd have sold my screenplay. Damn. *If only my agent hadn't died.*"

Pam was always blaming her dead screenplay career on her dead screenplay agent—and telling me how lucky I was for having a living, breathing, book agent. I encouraged her to stop her blame and start her search for a screenplay agent who had a better health regime. Or sell her screenplays herself. I reminded her how many of my book projects were sold without my book agent. Mine at that time, although *living*, wasn't doing much to help me *make a living.*

After a few initial publishing rejections of *How To Make Your Man Behave in 21 Days or Less Using the Secrets of Professional Dog Trainers*, he had backed away from the project. Not me. Not only did I doggedly work at selling that little book—I did so with pitbull dogged determination, sending it out *for nearly a year* to publishers on my own.

One day I had a meeting at *Playboy* to talk about writing an article on female masturbation (hey, I'm always ready to try my hand at anything—so to speak). Bruce, the editor, had just sold a humor book about babies. We got to talking, and I showed him my mockup of my "doggie" book, which I'd brought to the meeting—keeping in mind my YOU NEVER KNOW PRINCIPLE. Bruce grabbed Alice, the fiction editor, and showed her my book. She silently flipped through it, and succinctly said. "It's good. Send it to my friend over at Workman."

I did. It was sold. Yes, *Playboy* magazine—a publication that objectifies women—helped sell a book that objectifies men—plus, helped to prove that my YOU NEVER KNOW PRINCIPLE pays off—as does my principle:

> *When you waste time on blame,*
> *you miss the whole game.*

After all, had I been busily blaming, blaming, blaming my book agent for how this book was not being shopped around, and how my career was going to remain at a standstill because my agent was not getting things moving, I would have become a *martyr* instead of choosing to act *smarter*, and finding a publisher on my own. In fact, my entire career would be entirely different if I allowed myself to get caught up in the Blame Game—like Derrick, a photographer I know.

Derrick was always getting into fights with clients and assistants and reps—and losing business deals. *Everyone* he came into contact with he proclaimed to be an asshole—or a jealous asshole. He explained how everyone was out to get him because they were jealous of how good-looking he was. He never looked at a thing called CAUSE and EFFECT. Meaning: He never looked at his contribution to the commotion that went into motion around him. And so the same problems kept repeating themselves over and over—like *Groundhog Day: The Career Version.* Suddenly photo reps at *Glamour, Mademoiselle,* and *New York* magazine would mysteriously stop calling. He'd explain how these women were all moody, argumentative, bitchy—and how they all wanted to sleep with him. Every day Derrick would complain—over and over—how he was a slave to circumstance. (Actually, this is one way to differentiate a slave from a master: Bad things always seem to happen to slaves.) Derrick foolishly kept thinking the way to improve his business relations was to find new business relationships, but it was his relationship with blame that needed to change. He needed to stop operating under the slave principle:

If at first you don't succeed, it's someone else's fault

Derrick's not alone in his need to operate under this Slave Mentality. Al Capone did as well.

"I have spent the best years of my life," said Al, "giving people the lighter pleasures, helping them have a good time, and all I get is abuse, the existence of a hunted man." Yes, Capone was unable to take responsibility for his crimes and instead viewed himself as a misappreciated victim, a slave to circumstance. Like that photographer Derrick, he needed to take responsibility for his actions.

Sure enough, when I finally helped Derrick to see the part he played in his bad relationships, and showed him how he should be treating his photo editors more kindly, finally his career started to improve. He even got some of these photo editors back as clients.

Contrarily, a domintarix of one's destiny consciously chooses never to blame career dissatisfaction on others—or on childhood in retrospect, or on Mercury in retrograde. A dominatrix knows that blame can lead to major paralysis of one's career. When you're overly busy pinning responsibility for your failure on other people, you become too busy to move forward. For instance, imagine the following movie scene: Two bad guys are trying to rob a bank. Mid-robbery, the alarm goes off. They suddenly start arguing:

"It's *your* fault."

"No, it's *your* fault!"

They stand around the vault wasting precious minutes, instead of making their 3 o'clock meeting with the getaway car. This Blame Game won't get them anywhere—except jail.

Believe me, I understand the temptation to blame. Self-righteousness is a highly satisfying hobby. But you must resist it. After all, this is the deal on blame:

> *If you don't take responsibility for the bad stuff, then you lose your right to take credit for the good stuff.*

When you choose to blame, you give away your power to this other person. And a master never gives away power. If you blame your coworker for a project that goes wrong, you're basically saying: "It was her project—all I did was staple." All this does is make you look weak—and eliminates any potential of good that might come out of it in the future. Remember: Wise bosses know that failed projects can often make someone an "expert" in a certain area just as much as successful ones can—they will recognize your contribution and probably turn to you for advice the next time a similar issue arises.

If you want to be the master of your destiny, then you must know 110 percent that *you are fully responsible for everything in your life—both the good and the bad.* You must know 120 percent: *"I have what I have—and don't have what I don't have—all because of who I am."* In other words, you must take responsibility for your life—which requires (ugh) maturity—a quality a slave is lacking.

Don't Let a Blame Preoccupation Ruin Your Occupation

The blame habit is not an easy one to break, but it can—and *must*—be broken. Brain researchers say 95 percent of the thoughts you will have today are the same as those you had yesterday. It's up to you to *lower* that percentage at least a few points, and thereby *increase* your percentage probability for success. You can do this by CONSCIOUSLY deciding to look at your tendency to blame, knowing that until you take self-responsibility, you are doomed to live out *same shit, different outfit*. Meaning . . . from day to month to year the style of your clothes may change, but the style of your circumstances and problems won't.

When Blame Has Another Name

Margaret, a graphic designer, had a boss, Larry, who she thought was practically the equivalent of Darth Vader. Soon the truth revealed itself: Larry *was* in fact Darth Vader. He had a volcanic temper that erupted erratically—often in front of clients, thereby humiliating Margaret. She had a right to name Larry as the cause for her career dissatisfaction—at least for the first four or five months on the job. After that, the blame reverted back to her because:

If you can't cut out the blame, then cut those losses!

If your job sucks, and it looks like the sucking won't go away, you must ask yourself why *you* won't go away. Why stay with a sucky job—when you can at least find a new sucky job. (Just kidding.) But seriously, after a reasonable time passes (six months or 60 hours of complaining over 60 margaritas, whichever comes first), if you have not proactively done anything to change your circumstances, you relinquish your right to blame.

Today's Fantasy Role-Playing Exercises
(and Tips for Cracking Whips)

Avoid Bonding with Those Who Revel in Binds

There's a breed of people in every office who breed problems around them—ratfinking about your long lunch breaks, revealing confidential salary information, blaming everyone for every error. They're often seen in the office of higher-ups waving blame-of-others in their hand. You know who these people are—hopefully *not* because *you* are one of them. ANYWAY . . . these people are human Kryptonite. Make a list of them and entitle it the Most Unwanted List.

Mythtakes

Do you overhear yourself explaining away your career problems with mythical generalizations, shackled in stereotypes that, face it, are not true anymore? (Okay, so there may be some exceptions.) For instance: "I'm being held back because I'm too old." Or: "They don't want me on this high-powered project because I don't have an MBA." Or: "I'm being treated poorly because I am a woman." If so, set yourself free from these limiting beliefs. Remember: Career success depends more on maintaining a Master Mentality than it does on statistics. To help break free of these shackling thoughts that bind you—and blind you— write up a motivational list of people you know who are mythtake-breakers.

Your Current State of Unfairs

*L*ist your present grumble-grumble complaints about your career. Now, this might hurt, but accept the following: Some part of you attracted these complaints. All cause starts at a mental level. Thoughts are creative. Thoughts are energy. Over time, you attract what you think about. The world *around you* is a physical manifestation of the world *within you*. In other words, the world is your mirror—and it's one of those wraparound mirrors that catches you from every angle. There is no hiding. It reflects the behind-the-scene view you can't see—or don't want to see. If you feel angry, you attract people who make you feel anger. If you feel stupid, you attract people who make you feel stupid. If you feel successful, you attract people who make you feel successful. Therefore it's essential to BEAT ALL YOUR NEGATIVE THOUGHTS, OR ELSE IN TIME THEY'LL BEAT YOU. So list three situations where you blame another person. Now list five new alternative cause-and-effect explanations.

Master Card

*W*henever you feel like a Blame Brain, command your brain to fantasize about your long-term career goal—and, in particular, imagine your new business card with your new title. Now feel what you feel when you hand that card to someone. It's a law of the universe that how you think and feel on the inside will eventually show up on the outside. Whatever you believe with great feeling has no choice but to eventually become reality. HENCE MY USE OF CAPITAL LETTERS *and italics to again remind you to make sure your long-term goal plays a dominant role in the fight against blame.*

The Pooper-Scooper Factor

*C*ertain day-to-day frustrations are *nobody's fault.* They just happen. For instance, a broken Xerox machine delays a meeting or an innocent miscommunication creates a misprinting of a document. In other words, it's like this: You know how getting a puppy at first glance seems like 100 percent fun, but also comes with daily frustrations—like pooper-scoopering? Well, you must recognize that there are daily pooper-scooper aspects to all careers, as well.

Zen and the Art of Computer Blaming

I believe the problems you have with an inanimate object like a computer can reveal the role you play in the problems you have with people. For example, do you rush to bitch about a computer glitch when you may be at fault because of one of the following:

1. You didn't read the instructions fully before rushing in to use your computer.
2. You applied operating instructions that you learned from using another brand of computer to this particular computer.
3. You didn't check to see if the batteries are low and you need to take the time to recharge them
4. You are not performing routine preventive maintenance checkups to ensure smooth operation.

If you relate to any of the above, these problems could be symbolic clues to understanding the dynamic you are instigating with colleagues, employees, and bosses. Often the micro is the macro—and that goes for microchip, as well.

master mantras to help you whip

Blame

into submission

Next time you're ready to haul out the blame, halt and remember:

1. I am not a SLAVE who immediately points the finger at another person. I am a MASTER who sees the whole other hand of self-responsibility.

2. I am not a SLAVE who thinks everyone is out to get me. I am a MASTER who goes out and gets what I want.

3. I am not a SLAVE to circumstance. I am a MASTER of my destiny.

4. I am not a SLAVE who gets tossed around by others like a leaf in the wind. I am a MASTER who holds firmly to the belief that I can win.

5. I am not a SLAVE who gets all tied up in what others do and say. I am a MASTER who believes in free will—and knows free will comes with a price at times.

Whip

Impatience

Into Submission

or

I Want More—and Faster

I f you want to torture someone, make him wait. Waiting is hell. In fact, I think waiting to see if you are going to hell or not is far more torturous than actually *being* there. So much so that if you really want to curse someone out, don't tell him "Go to hell!" Tell him "Go wait to see if you're going to hell."

Unfortunately, there exists a standard business equivalent of this sentence, which is: "We'll get back to you." And in advertising there is an alternate version called: "Let's do a focus group and decide." A focus group is a roundtable discussion that is set up among people gathered in a mall, bribed with free food, to debate what they think about a particular commercial-in-the-making. Often focus groups work like de-focus groups. They gather so many opinions that the end result is mass confusion—and fodder for impatience because nothing moves forward.

For instance, one year my art director's wife found out she was pregnant the same time we were assigned to create a commercial. Thanks to the de-focusing effects of focus groups, my art director's wife gave birth long before the final ad was actually shot. In other words, it takes longer to produce a TV commercial than a live human being. AND, in *other* other words:

*Everything has its process.
You must respect the process.*

A baby takes nine months to be born (more or less). Impatience will not speed up birth production, no matter how much the parents want that baby in their lives. Nor will it speed up commercial production—no matter how much you want the thing done and *out* of your life. If you let impatience influence you in business, you'll wind up in the long run in the wrong place. You'll cut corners, fudge numbers, and end up with a product that screams: "I was cheap and easy!" Basically, it's like this. There are always two reasons for doing anything:

1. The RIGHT reason.
2. The reason that is motivated by SPEED.

And there are always two reasons for choosing the second speed reason:

1. Need for CONTROL.
2. Feelings of DOUBT and INSECURITY.

When you learn to trust yourself and your talents and the process, you're on your way to success—even if it's a slower path to success. When it comes to impatience, you should always keep in mind:

1. Fast doesn't always last.
2. A shortcut is often the longest distance between two points.
3. It's always better to go for long-term greed over short-term greed.

For example, consider the following people:

Meema, a film director, was at first tempted to try to quickly make the Sundance Festival deadline and enter her documentary *Breasts* before it was edited fully. But despite the potential for exposure to key distributors there, she decided to forgo slapping something together, and let *Breasts* blossom further, until it got to a more developed place. Once she had a product she was thrilled with and had a lot of confidence in, she then showed it to HBO, and got herself a deal. *And now* it's also available on video—check it out!

Keith, a managing director at Commonwealth Associates, also respects life's varying ebbs and flows. "Many of of my clients want me to double their portfolios by the end of the week. I remind them to hold out until the right investment comes along, and not to buy too soon or sell too early. In my business having the patience to wait even a few hours translates into thousands of dollars—or more."

Bryan, a music producer, recognizes that you can't rush creating a good song. He waits until he finds the right team of musicians and gets it done right the first time. "Everything in life has a rhythm like music," says Bryan, "Everything has its own right timing."

Sir Isaac Newton agrees. He said: "If I have done the public any service it is due to patient thought."

ASAP's Fables

We're all lazy. We all want it easy. We all want to believe we can get great things done with the least effort. But a dominatrix of one's destiny recognizes this is rarely the case. A lot of one's career life can be like watching Jell-O set. Slow and tedious. Usually, writing a great business report, editing a great film, or producing a great song *takes great time.* Getting impatient won't help. (If only anxiety speeded things up, I'd be so much further ahead.)

I believe a test of one's strength of character all comes down to:

The famous marshmallow test question.

Would you rather have one marshmallow now or two marshmallows later?

Personally I would go for two now—and five later. But that's just me—or at least that's the old me—which is really the young me, versus the new me which is the older—and wiser—me. The old-young Karen's motto used to be:

I want more—and faster.

The new-older-wiser Karen has lived (more slowly) and learned (quickly) that in the same way a smart movie actor knows to patiently wait until the right "two marshmallow" movie project comes along rather than grab at the first "one marshmallow" high-paying grade B film and wind up with a grade B career, it pays for *all business people—writers, doctors, lawyers, accountants, mimes—you name it—to wait for the right "two marshmallow" business opportunity.*

And the secret to building up one's patience level is to work on building up one's self-esteem and enthusiasm for one's long-term goal.

For instance, when I left advertising, I was at first a little impatient about the long, tedious "two marshmallow" book writing/selling process. During this same time an entrepreneur dangled the temptation of setting me up as president of my own immediate "one marshmallow" small ad agency—yet another version of the career I'd just left in hopes of writing "two marshmallow" books. The IMPATIENT me, THE *INSECURE* ME, THE NOW *POORER* ME, found this alluring. I could develop ad campaigns in my sleep. BUT, as you can tell—because you are reading this "two marshmallow" book—I held out for the writing career. I reminded myself how much I longed to write provocative, funny, inspiring books, then reminded myself about how I felt I had the goods to deliver, and thereby had the patience to hold out for my LONG-TERM GOAL—and am a happier gal for it.

Basically, developing patience not only promises more money, satisfaction, and marshmallows, but more inner peace. Or, as that underappreciated Zen philosopher Bazooka Joe reminds us: "Patience is a virtue. Seersucker is a fabric."

Today's Fantasy Role-Playing Exercises
(and Tips for Cracking Whips)

Unrestraining Orders

*J*ust as things come out different in a microwave than in a conventional oven, things also come out different in a speeded-up work project—and not usually the "good" kind of different. So right now, ask yourself: Are you rushing a work project—or letting someone else rush you? If so, remember SPEED KILLS. (I'm talking about trying to *speed up* work. Though I don't recommend the other speed, either. I once did speed to try to lose weight. All it did was make me eat faster.)

ANYWAY . . . For willpower to slow yourself down, stare at the second hand on your watch for 60 seconds. This exercise works like meditation, hypnotically slowing down your inner freneticism.

Wait Lifting

What is that one thing you are waiting for right now that is driving you batty? It could be feedback on a report you gave your boss *two weeks ago*, or an assignment you and your department were supposed to be working on that's turning into Chinese Water Torture. Now promise yourself that every time an impatient wave of thought flickers through your brain about having to wait for these things, you will command your mind not to think about it for the next five minutes. Then increase your patience level another five minutes. Then another five minutes. If you keep raising your wait quotient, in time you'll strengthen your patience muscles.

Fast Talk

What inner monologue goes through your head when you feel impatient? Think about whether this inner monologue comes from someone you know. For instance, could this monologue be a MOM-O-LOGUE, criticisms your mom used to level against you like: "I thought I told you I wanted this done *yesterday*, young lady!" If so, recognize this voice in your head—and talk back to it.

Stalk, Don't Run

....

*J*ust like animals know how to stalk prey, you too can use the art of stalking, whether it's with a potential client or buyer or new employer. In other words, you must recognize the benefits of patiently holding out for a good deal. Timing is everything in negotiation, so you must, like an animal, get intuitively tuned to how impatient the other guy is to get the deal done—and know that if someone is impatient, you have a lot more bargaining power.

Time Travel a Year Into the Future

....

*R*emember: Whatever the mind believes is real will eventually—with patience—manifest itself. So, whenever you're feeling impatient about the speed at which your career is traveling, translate your dreams from future tense to present tense. Instead of: "I will be the VP of my division sometime next year," say "I *am* the VP." Instead of: "I will try to take responsibility for this high-profile project at some point." Say: "I *own* this project—and everyone knows it." Envision where your career will be a year from now, and remain focused on this BIGGER, BETTER, JUICER, NOW-WITH-MORE-FLAVOR-THAN-EVER FUTURE.

A Dominant Rule of the Universe

....

*A*ccept the following permanent condition of life: Everything always takes three times as long as you think—and costs twice as much.

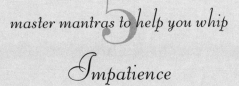

master mantras to help you whip

Impatience

into submission

1. I am not a SLAVE who wishes life moved faster. I am a MASTER of the belief that slow-and-steady wins the promotions.

2. I am not a SLAVE who cannot enjoy the journey. I am a MASTER who knows how to relax and enjoy the ride to the top.

3. I am not a SLAVE who gobbles down one marshmallow now. I am a MASTER who holds out for two marshmallows—then winds up getting six or seven.

4. I am not a SLAVE who wants things now. I am a MASTER who lives and works in the now, getting things done, so I have a better future later.

5. I am not a SLAVE who expects overnight success in an hour. I am a MASTER who recognizes that overnight success might take a few extra weeks, but it's a-comin', it's a-comin'.

Whip

Procrastination

Into Submission

or

....

You Must Act—or Be Acted Upon

....

Confession: You know that if I'm vacuuming, I have an important work project due—because I *hate* to vacuum.

Plus I don't even have carpeting.

I'm a master at procrastinating. (If only I could apply my talent for impatience that I mentioned in yesterday's chapter to the things that I'm tempted to procrastinate about, which—ho boy—are many.)

You know what? For this particular discussion I feel I should break the mold from chapters past. Instead of advising HOW NOT TO procrastinate, I feel, because I am such an expert, that I'm better qualified to give tips on:

How to be a master procrastinator.

Besides my devotion to the ol' Hoover, I personally also recommend the telephone, though the distracting elements of food are not to be underappreciated. I often like to combine these two, and use the phone to order up food—then talk on the phone while eating.

Procrastination comes in many forms, and not just the obvious push-button and rotary options. When you stop to think about it—like stopping *right now*—don't start procrastinating on me!—many of our negative emotions serve as Procrastinatory Aids. For example: WORRY, ANGER, and DEPRESSION can all stop you from moving forward. Plus, there's also COMPLAINING and INDECISION, which can both work to keep you away from work. And then there's PERFECTIONISM, which is procrastination all gussied up to look real purty. ("As long as my apartment/desk/new suit is spotless, we can avoid the fact that I'm late, right?") Basically, procrastination is a master of disguise—that is, from the slave's POV. But a master of one's destiny can see through procrastination—and thereby see her way through it—which I am now mastering the art of doing.

Master Your Feelings, Master Your Dealings

The first step to fighting back against procrastination is to recognize all your fancy alibis, lies, bad habits, and excuses that prevent you from accomplishing your work goals.

Now take me. I have now cut back on the vacuuming. I ultimately recognized it was about my fear of success—plus, neither my bleached oak wood floors nor my adoring editor Suzanne Oaks could take it anymore. ANYWAY, I've found that this nonvacuuming vacuum has created more time and energy to finish this book. I've also since cut back on the telephone calls and food delivery and finished my screenplay.

Betsy, a Web designer, has confessed she relates to my procrastinatory habits. She would spend hours surfing the Internet, rationalizing to herself that she was "researching" Web designs for future projects. "I would jump from site to site, and wind up not designing my own site assignments. Then finally a client got really angry that I was behind on my deadlines and I realized how I was procrastinating. I guess I was afraid of not doing an impressive job, but then I recognized, ironically, my fears were becoming self-fulfilling because of all the surfing I was doing. So now I allow myself only one hour a day."

Work Now, Procrastinate Later

Often procrastination is about FEAR OF FAILURE—or its separated-at-birth twin, FEAR OF SUCCESS. It's often hard to tell these two fears apart. However, both fear of success and fear of failure have the same cure: *You must command your mind to remember all the reasons that you are talented at performing the skills required—and why you have passion for the end result—your long-term goal.*

Marcia, a painter, applies these cures for greater success. Marcia admits there are many days she doesn't feel inspired to work. "On these days, I go to a musem and see the masters, and get revved up by their talent and passion—and remind myself how much I'd love to be on a museum or gallery wall some day."

Marcia is acting on—and benefiting from—what Emerson once said: "A man becomes what he thinks about most of the time." (Which I guess in my case means that I am becoming a cheeseburger with fries.)

ANYWAY, overcoming procrastination is a true test of one's character, and a test of one's integrity to stay true to one's passions—which can be hard to sustain as time moves on. But a master knows—as Principle #11 states—that *to whip your career into submission you must keep yourself in a constant state of excitement.* Meaning:

Better titillate than never.

You must keep fanning the fires of your soul's passions long after that titillating honeymoon period of your initial job assignment has passed. As Ralph Waldo Emerson said: *"Nothing great was ever achieved without enthusiasm."* Or maybe he said *"without lots of cappuccino."* No, no, it was enthusiasm. ANYWAY . . . David, President of Good Stuff, a toy company, knows how to be a master of his enthusiasm.

David explains, "I make toys and games for a living, because I love games. So I play a game with myself every time a tough work project or problem arises. I set a time limit for fixing the problem, and see it as a fun challenge, thereby fighting my tendency for procrastination."

David recognizes an important truth about procrastination. Basically:

Time mastery = Career mastery

Aristotle called this: "We are what we repeatedly do."

Meaning, if I want to be a vacuumer/telephone talker/cheeseburger eater, then suck and chat and chew I must do. However, if I want to be a successful writer, then I must write, damn it.

Today's Fantasy Role-Playing Exercises
(and Tips for Cracking Whips)

Lobster Newjob

How do you eat a lobster? Do you save the best parts for last or eat them right away? This is most likely how you deal with your workload. A good trick to deal with procrastination: Do the worst part of your job first—deal with your tedious expense reports, or number crunch that budget so it's client-friendly. Afterward, you can reward yourself with the better parts of your job. Apply this technique to your work today.

Right Time, Wrong Pace

*D*o you keep waiting for the time to be right to start a project? If so, you must recognize that hesitation is an enemy of success. Although timing is everything, it's not EVERY-THING. If you keep waiting, the timing may never be right. You must learn to just go ahead and start where you stand. There's a Zen quote: "A journey of 1,000 miles must begin with a single step." You must work with what you have, and keep stepping it up further as you go along. So today pick a deadline for starting an assignment you've been avoiding, write it in your calender, and stick to it.

All Talk, a Lot of Action

*T*ell people out loud what you plan to accomplish. If you spread the word, it's harder to back out of doing it because you'll know these people will ask you about it later. I mean, do you really want to tell people, "No, I didn't have time to look over those financial statements because I was too busy . . . vacuuming?" Plus, sometimes talking about a project can help REIGNITE YOUR PASSION about the good, exciting aspects of a job—the kind of details you tell people about—that can sometimes get overlooked if you're focusing on the more mundane stuff.

Pleasure in Your Pain

One of the big reasons people procrastinate is to avoid what they see as pain. So what you must do is FIND THE *PLEASURE* IN YOUR PAIN. Focus on the pleasure that will come when you accomplish your goals. For instance, do as Marcia the painter does when she does not want to paint on a given day: She envisions her finished, fabulous painting hanging on the wall in a gallery, and it's that payoff for all her hard work that keeps her cranking instead of cranky. Remind yourself right now of what your end pleasure will be. Every time you want to procrastinate, let this PLEASURE DOMINATE your thoughts.

Photo Finish

Find photos from magazines of the end results you want to attain—even (and especially) materialistic end results: a sports car, a motorcycle, a spa vacation, whatever. Heck, sometimes you just can't be motivated by all that deep philosophical stuff. However, superficial motivations nearly always seem to do the trick.

Hate Prevents Late

Think of a competitor or enemy you have in your life. Every time you want to procrastinate, envision this person rooting you on to procrastinate so you will thereby be less successful. This should help you resist your resistance to work, and tap into your inner strength.

Daily Dilly Dally

What are your favorite Procrastinatory Aids—the telephone, TV, fly fishing, complaining, reading this book? (*Wait!* I take back that last one.) Pick one a day to get rid of— or at least replace it with a procrastinatory act that will reinspire you to perform. If you're a movie producer, go see a movie. If you're a stockbroker, go read the *Wall Street Journal.*

See It as Growing Not Groaning

In the movie *Karate Kid*, the Zen master helped his pupil build up his character by having him scrub floors. Each day it's good to do at least one small thing you do not want to do: shine your shoes or clean your desk. Setting up these little victories for yourself will help you build up your personal sense of power for accomplishing larger goals.

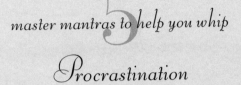

master mantras to help you whip

Procrastination

into submission

1. I am not a SLAVE who puts things off. I am MASTER who gets things going.

2. I am not a SLAVE whose favorite time of day is "later." I am a MASTER who knows: *"Later does not exist. Only now exists. And now is where my power lies."*

3. I am not a SLAVE who fears failure and thereby procrastinates. I am a MASTER who uses my fear of failure to make sure I won't procrastinate.

4. I am not a SLAVE who sees happiness as avoiding difficult work. I am a MASTER who knows happiness is all about achieving goals.

5. I am not a SLAVE who doesn't move forward because I dread the 1,000 miles ahead of me. I am a MASTER who starts one step at a time to travel these 1,000 miles.

Whip

Listening Problems

Into Submission

or

When You Listen for the Thunder,
You're Not Surprised by the Lightning

D on't ever try to watch the movie *Babe* on video while cleaning up your apartment. I tried to do this once. The result? I wasn't able to follow the story-line of this simple, little man-meets-pig, man-saves-pig-from-becoming-Christmas-dinner, pig-wins-sheep-herding-contest movie plot because I was trying to do too many things at once. (Now how *did* this pig make the career switch from bacon to hero?)

One's career life can work like this—or rather *not* work like this. And unfortunately in our careers we don't have rewind and replay. Well, we do. But it means you have to redo the assign-ment—or relearn the lesson.

Have You Heard?

few years ago I was worried I was losing my memory. A client had told me she expected some headlines on Thursday. I didn't remember that conversation at all. Then my girlfriend Phyllis called me up, miffed. She was waiting for me to call her back after I got off call waiting. I remembered her telling me *she'd* call *me* back. ANYWAY . . . I thought maybe I had an iron deficiency or some dreaded disease that was creating memory loss. Then I realized I was suffering from my *Babe* Video Syndrome. I was trying to do too many things at once and was NOT FULLY LISTENING.

The good news was: My brain and its memory storage system worked just fine.

The bad news was: I was just being plain ol' rude.

Since then I've improved my listening skills. For instance, I now take notes on the phone when people call me, and repeat back what they say. It's working. The proof? The other day these techniques enabled me to hear the following story from Carol, a stylist.

Carol was always overbooked, juggling three or four jobs a week styling rock stars for album covers. One week she was trying to meet five different deadlines, and she didn't hear her client tell her one of her styling jobs had been postponed. So she did more work than she needed to do because she wasn't *fully* listening.

The Scene and Heard

ay Bradbury, in his book *Farenheit 451*, describes a society where you MUST drive over 65 mph, so you cannot experience the world around you, and where there are no porches, so you cannot sit and think. Today's fast motion/commotion career scene is not so different from this science fiction, since our business world provides a similar frenetic environment. Most companies seem to foster that same 65 mph and over mentality, with speed-to-market cycles, and fast-turnaround inventory all becoming the "MORE! SOONER! FASTER!" mantras of corporate life. Unfortunately, we often translate this high-metabolism thinking into high consumption of tasks and busy work. We can keep so busy we don't fully listen to what bosses and clients and colleagues are trying to communicate to us—which translates into bad business.

Forget My Sex Drive. Pay Attention to my Need-to-Be-Listened-to Drive

*I*n our quest to do more, more, more, we forget that we all crave someone to listen intently to us. Hence people talk to their dogs—and God. Both are especially good audiences—not only because they'll patiently sit and listen, but because we know they won't interrupt. And when/if you think God is not fully listening, then you'll probably stop talking to God for a while. In fact, I believe the success of the vast array of 900 numbers—from sex lines to psychic operators—is due more to our need *to be listened to* than it is to hear what the heck the other person has to say back to us afterward.

Dale Carnegie, in his book *How To Win Friends and Influence People*, recognizes the power and influence a good listener has on clients and bosses in business. He promises that once you improve your listening skills, more people will seek out your company, and your personal contacts will increase. In particular, he also warns against:

Talkus interruptus.

Interrupting someone who is talking to make a point will only worsen your position in the argument. Carnegie enthusiastically advises to always wait until your conversation mate has

completely finished his point—even asking him if he's done—
before you make your own point—WHICH REQUIRES MUCH
DISCIPLINE. Just ask Fran Lebowitz, author of *Metropolitan
Life.* She once quipped: "The opposite of talking isn't listening,
it's waiting." However, Carnegie promises that a person who listens 110 percent actively without interrupting will live up to the
promise of his book title, and garner a good title for his business
card.

Another Mistress Karen listening trick is to listen in business
the way I listen when I'm interviewing people for a magazine article. For instance, one time I was writing a piece on male escorts
for *Marie Claire.* I had to go undercover, and gather all kinds of
wild details about these hunky guys' lives—without the aid of a
tape recorder. I suddenly became the best little listener—plus it
helped that these guys were SEXY AS ALL GET-OUT.

You should try this some time. No, not talking to male escorts. I mean pretending the person you're in a meeting with is
someone you have to write about later and quote. You'll find you
have to:

*Try on the following as a
good hearing aid.*

1. Close your mouth.
2. Open your ears.
3. Open your eyes.
4. Open your mind.

We've already covered #1 and #2. Now about #3, opening
your eyes. I believe:

*You can use your sight to hear better
in two different ways.*

1. By making good eye contact, you'll encourage your
   conversation mate to relax and talk more freely,

and thereby you'll gather more valuable business data.

2. By keeping an eye out for all the body language, you'll gather more valuable personal data that will help you in dealing with this person in business. (In fact, studies have shown that as much as 83 percent of sensory communication comes from our eyes, not our ears. Hence it's always important to *listen with your eyes.*)

The more personal data you gather, the more you can understand a person's motivations—and the more you understand a person's motivations, the more you can influence him in business dealings. You must always:

Know thy audience.

Jackie Mason once told me that he never does the same comedy act twice. When he heads out on stage, he first throws out a few test jokes to see what kind of audience he has that night— *then he listens to their response* and responds with specific humor appropriate for each individual audience.

You, too, must do this. You must learn to read people's operating instructions *before* you start giving them instructions— by opening not only your ears, but *your eyes.*

Now, about #4: opening your mind. This means you have to make sure it's not only open but *empty* of all expectations, otherwise you'll be so busy listening for what *you expect to hear,* that you might miss out on *new, pertinent information.* The Buddhists have a saying about this: "In the beginner's mind there are many possibilities. In the expert's mind there are few."

Which reminds me of an old Buddhist fable:

Dead Wrong

A man came home to find his house burned to the ground. His son, whom he had left inside, was nowhere to be found, and everyone in the village assumed he was dead in the ashes. HOWEVER, in reality the house had been burned down by a wacky infertile couple who stole the boy and took him to their small house deep in the woods, where the son lived for five years—until he escaped. During this time, the boy's father greatly mourned the boy's tragic death, and was at home staring at a slightly burned photo he still had, when the son, having trekked for months through the labyrinth of woods, finally found his way back to where his father was now living. Excitedly, the son knocked on the door. "Who's there?" asked his father. "It is me, your son," the son exclaimed. "I have returned!" The man thought this was some sadistic prankster: "Go away!" he yelled. "My son is dead!" The boy knocked again, and yelled, "But I am your son, father! I have returned! I am alive!" "Go away!" the father again yelled. "My son is dead!" And this dialogue repeated itself. Again. And again. Until the father, crying and still staring at the son's photo, went upstairs. The boy continued to knock until morning, when he finally went away—never to return.

In business this story translates into not hearing about a better business opportunity: a reemerging-from-the-rubble-heap stock if you're a stockbroker, or a new, improved kind of fabric, if you're a fashion designer. The moral of all these stories, folks?

Don't Let Your Convictions Become Your Restrictions

*H*aving an open mind also means being open to learning from everyone, not only your colleagues, but your secretary, your taxi driver, your mother, your child, that stranger on the airplane. I once was seated beside a man who was into gardening, and he unwittingly gave me some Zen wisdom that helped encourage me to leave advertising for my writing career:

"The secret to becoming a good gardener," he said, "is to accept that some plants are only meant to live a certain time or season. If you try to make them live longer than that you will be a bad gardener."

You never know where good business philosophies will come from.

Though at the same time you have to watch out that you're not just listening wide-eyed and bushy-tailed to any muttering idiot—or listening only for what you *want* to hear.

Personally, I've always found it helpful to purposefully seek out people to listen to that I know in advance will definitely teach me things. I like to find people who are at least five years ahead of me in their careers and get them to start blabbering about what they've learned. Or another tip: Next party you're at, don't automatically start turning your head to talk to that cute thing that's the center of attention. Look for the quiet, older person in the corner who has probably learned a lot about life from *observing*, not performing.

There's a Chinese proverb: "A single conversation across the table from a wise man is worth a month's study of books."

Today's Fantasy Role-Playing Exercises (and Tips for Cracking Whips)

Are You Card of Hearing?

*D*o something that shows you are listening. Send a thoughtful card to someone in business today.

Declare Independence Day

*D*o you have negative people in your life that you've been listening to? Or some clown you've been allowing to give you business advice? Declare your independence from them today.

Write a list of people you will not to listen to anymore—then listen to your promise not to listen to them.

Now with 40 Percent Less Filler

Today, decide you will talk 40 percent less than usual. See how much more you hear.

You Don't Say?

Usually people reveal who they truly are during "CUSP TIMES." Meaning? The post-meeting gab period. So pay attention to the clues you can receive after a long talk with a boss or a colleague. Listen for those "PRE-SUCKING SOUNDS"—cues that working with them might suck. For instance, I always watch out for what I call "Hyperbole People." These are folks who talk in hyperboles: "You're a genius." "That's fabulous." "This is the best report I've seen in my entire life—and a few of my past lives, as well."

Be a Recording Star

Tape record some of your phone conversations, and listen to yourself raptly. Decide if there's something about your communication style that needs changing. For instance, do you not let your conversation mate get a word in? If so, remember: Often it's more appealing to be *INTERESTED* than *INTERESTING*.

Read It and Reap

....

I recommend two books to improve your listening skills. First, Dale Carnegie's *How To Win Friends and Influence People* goes into great detail on how to be a better listener. For example, he stresses the importance of listening to a person's name when you first meet, and committing it to memory. Second, *The Male/Female Dictionary*, written by my friend Susan Shapiro. The book humorously helps men and women understand what the heck we're each saying to each other.

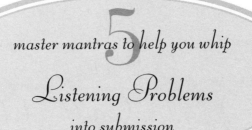

master mantras to help you whip

Listening Problems

into submission

Next time you feel like someone must have pressed the mute button on your career TV screen, remember:

1. I am not a SLAVE who unconsciously talks nonstop. I am a MASTER who consciously listens nonstop.

2. I am not a SLAVE who interrupts a person during the middle of a point. I am a MASTER who pointedly bites my tongue—even if this person's point is pointless.

3. I am not a SLAVE who looks around the conference room to see if there's any cheese Danish left. I am a MASTER who makes a contract to keep eye contact with whomever is speaking.

4. I am not a SLAVE who makes up my mind in advance who a person is and what a person will say. I am a MASTER who keeps open—open, open, open—ears, eyes, and mind.

5. I am not a SLAVE who listens 100 percent openly to 100 percent everyone. I am a MASTER who has the discipline to know whom to be open to.

DAY TWELVE

Whip Your Health Into Submission

or

You Must Eat and Drink to Be Merry

I believe the mind and body are one—except during PMS, when mind and body are about two and a half. If you want your mind to work at its peak, it pays to keep your body at its peak—and vice versa.

A lot of bad emotions—like anger and depression—come from the fact that you're not in perfect health, a very common problem among busy professional women in particular. There's a famous quote: *"Mens sana in corpore sano."* Or: "In a sound body rests a sound mind."

Which is a very sound awareness.

And although I've always known this advice, I haven't religiously followed it. I've even been a downright atheist about it at times. Up until a few years ago, whenever I was overwhelmed with work, I used to believe (aka: rationalize) that this meant I didn't have time to go to the gym and eat normal meals. Inevitably, this laissez-faire (aka: lazy flare) attitude led to decreased productivity: midday naps or mid-level quality work. I'd feel too bloated from the box of glazed donuts I'd devoured and the keg of coffee I'd glugged it down with to write anything resembling cohesive thought.

Then one day my friend David told me about how his life changed when he started working out in the mornings. I witnessed how he seemed more energetic—and was dressing in more expensive suits (due to his promotions) that fit him better (due to his new, perkier buns). I started joining him in the mornings and now I truly recognize that:

Taking time for fitness saves time.

The benefits of working out regularly (besides perkier buns) include the following:

1. More energy.
2. More enthusiasm.
3. More concentration.
4. More relaxed state of mind.
5. Fewer sick days.
6. Less required sleep.

Plus, I've found that when I work out in the morning I need to drink less coffee. Basically:

20 minutes on the stairmaster = 1 mochaccino + then some

I never thought I'd ever give up coffee. I was a total slave to caffeine. It represented one of my four basic breakfast food groups. The others being:

2. a bagel.
3. with jelly.
4. and butter.

Altogether all of this made for a very goofy dining experience.

It's like this: Coffee depletes your body of water and nutrition. And a bagel with jelly and butter gives your body zilcho nutrition. In fact, both coffee and carbos are known to give you a big energy high followed by a Grand Canyonesque plummet.

The trick is to feed your body foods that supply a more even flow of energy. In the morning, fruit is recommended by most nutritionists because it's so easy to digest. In the afternoons and evenings, nutritionists recommend that whatever you eat you include a salad, not only because a salad itself is good for you, but because it's good for the digestion of whatever else you're eating with it.

Extra Strength Placebos

I believe in vitamins. I know, I know some folks snicker about them. But I swear I've been taking some that I feel truly work. And even if they're placebos, they're damn good placebos—extra strength placebos. Whenever I've been faithful to my stable of organic health stabilizers, I'm full of vim and vigor and ready for a little career vipping . . . uh, rather, *whipping. Yeehaa!*

Okay, I'll share. Here it is:

Mistress Karen's Whip Your Career Fatigue Whippers

1. Greens Plus—everything your mother told you to eat in powder form.
2. Guarana—an herb from Brazil that gives you energy galore.

3. Ginseng—particularly the stuff from Siberia—it will totally make you more energetic and clearheaded. In fact, in one lab test, mice given ginseng swam 59 percent longer than the control group. I say: If it's good for mice, it's good for the rat race of your career.

4. Water—a miracle medicine. I try to drink eight to ten glasses a day. Water helps absorb nutrients and regulates electrolytes that allow your nerves to send signals to your brain.

5. Spirulina and blue green algae—we're talking major energy booster.

6. St. John's Wort—considered the Prozac of Europe.

I also try to make my main meals breakfast and lunch, and make dinner the lightest meal of the day. Emphasis on TRY. Emphasis on DISCIPLINE. And let me tell you I am no Kate Moss when it comes to discipline around food. In fact, I don't know if I envy Kate Moss. I mean, sure she has Johnny Depp, but she doesn't have deep dish Chicago-style pizza.

ANYWAY . . . I've found that the discipline I put into better eating habits leads to better health, better mood, better work, better paycheck—as well as the aformentioned better buns!

Speaking of buns . . . all too many of us busy career women can get confused and believe that just because we look damn swell on the outside, this means everything is in hunky dory condition on the inside. We mistakenly believe that if we're still getting checked out at the gym this means we don't have to go for check ups with our doctors. In a word: *wrongo!* We must not forget to have yearly exams physically, gynecologically, and dentally. For me the last one is easy. I have this gorgeous dentist, Gregg. Thanks to Gregg, I no longer fear dental exams. On the contrary, I even look forward to them. I have recently started to chomp Bubblelicious—a pack a day. (Though it figures I'd fall for a guy who could conceivably cause me pain. . . .)

Today's Fantasy Role-Playing Exercises
(and Tips For Cracking Whips)

What's Eating You?

Today, notice how your stomach feels after each meal. Are there certain foods that you eat by habit, but are making you *nauseous, tired, irritable, anxious?* If so, drop these foods like a hot potato. Are you getting enough protein in your regular diet? Nutritionists recommend a daily allotment the size of "two playing cards' worth" of meat or tofu. And what's the skinny on your fat intake? Although fat has gotten some bad PR, it's still a necessary evil. Fat circulates continuously in your blood, carrying Vitamins A, D, E, and K—plus it's needed to convert food to energy. So try to have two to three tablespoons of oil a day. Also, if it seems that no matter what you eat, you're always having digestion problems, consider that you need to slow down—or "SLOW UP" as I called it in a previous day's lesson.

Invest in Fresh Air Fun

Take a walk at some point during the day today. Breathe in the air. Become aware of the sky, the wind, and any plant life you can manage to find around you. Buy yourself flowers for the office.

Get Rubbed the Right Way

*S*chedule a massage for yourself this week. It will help you relax both your mind and body simultaneously.

Find the Pleasure in Your Pain

*W*rite a list of all the benefits you'd receive if you worked out daily. Every time you think of the pain of working out consult this list of pleasures to cheerlead you on.

Wheaties for the Brain

*Y*ou must condition your mind like an athlete would his body. A lot of fatigue is about not disciplining your brain to resist negative thoughts. Today try to make sure that the thoughts you feed your synapses are positive morsels and uplifting tidbits. And for some good "thought for food," buy a copy of Reverend Norman Vincent Peale's *The Power of Positive Thinking*. It's full of stories about people who improved their mental diets and became masters of their destiny.

If You Want Your Body to Be Smoking, You've Got to Stop Smoking!

*G*ood health is all about self-mastery—and not just when it comes to exercise and food, but also *cigarettes*. There are some women who are obsessive about the Stairmaster and committed to vegetarianism—but who still *light up*. If you're one of these cigaretteaholics, find a chain of smokers to join forces with and support one another to cut out this self-destructive habit.

Play Doctor

Make a doctor's appointment today for yourself—and make sure every part of you is in working order from your head to toes.

master mantras to help you whip

Your Health

into submission

Next time you're feeling sick and tired of feeling sick and tired, remember:

1. I am not a SLAVE who sleeps late into the morning. I am a MASTER who doesn't let sleeping dogs lie and rises early to work out.

2. I am not a SLAVE who restrains myself with limited negative thinking. I am a MASTER who unshackles negative beliefs so I can run loose and freely in the career field of my choosing.

3. I am not a SLAVE who eats gobs of sugar. I am a MASTER who knows life is sweeter without it.

4. I am not a SLAVE who wakes up and thinks negative thoughts. I am a MASTER who makes up my mind to think positively.

5. I am not a SLAVE who never has time for my health. I am a MASTER who knows that taking time for my health now saves sick days later.

Whip

Your Money Situation

Into Submission

or

....

Money Talks—and It Often Says "Later!"

....

few years ago I snagged a freelance gig as a creative director for TNT. When the client asked me how much money I wanted, I included in my fee an extra salary for an assistant art director, then doubled the total so as to have bargaining leverage.

Guess what?

The client accepted my inflated whopping salary suggestion.

Guess what else?

This salivating salary, so it turned out, did *not* even include an art director. TNT wanted to supply its own. Meaning: TNT was paying me *four* times what I expected. (Yeehaa!)

That's when I realized:

Sometimes, all you gotta do is ask.

I'd noticed this strategy before in my career. As I mentioned, the more I wanted *out* of advertising, the more my salary went *up.* Since I wasn't afraid of losing my job, I wasn't afraid to ask for fees with lots of zeros in them. The cash-and-carry lesson to take to the bank?

If You Position Yourself as a Big League Player, You Don't Have to Settle for a Little League Salary

There's an old saying: "It's not who you are that holds you back, but what you think you're not." If I had hemmed and hawed about what I thought I was worth when I was asking for these humongous amounts of money, I would have lost the confidence needed to do a Big Time Negotiation. Instead, I went into the situation focused on what I had to offer—*not* on what might be wrong with me and my salary demands. I believe this is one of the reasons that old saying "The rich get richer" is true. Because the rich don't think of themselves as "not rich," they attract money a-plenty to themselves.

You, too, must stop thinking of yourself as being stuck with a certain ceiling on your earnings. If you're walking around feeling as if you'll *never* make over $40,000 a year, well then, so be it. Chances are that $40,000 will be your mental credit line that your mind will attract and lend to you this year from the universe's vast, abundant money source. However, if you truly want a raise from your present $40,000-a-year salary, then you must first raise your prosperity consciousness. You must become aware that *there is a vast and abundant source of money out there in this world,* and believe fully that some of it has your name on it—and if your name is Benjamin Franklin, then a lot of it has your name on it.

And if your name is Deepak Chopra, then you'll do pretty darn good in the money department as well.

In his book *Creating Affluence: Wealth Consciousness in the Field of All Possibilities,* Deepak Chopra discusses how "affluence is our natural state" and how we must re-learn how to become aware that "the entire physical universe with all its abundance is the offspring of an unbounded, limitless field of all possibilities."

Chopra believes that all we must do is "re-learn" how to tap into this field of abundance.

I'll tell you what. Let's translate the above spiritualese into Karenese: Basically what Chopra is saying is that you must believe in the principle:

I Think, Therefore . . . I Have.

SO, IF YOU WANNA MAKE GOBS OF MONEY, THE FIRST STEP IS TO MAKE THE DECISION: "I *AM* GOING TO MAKE GOBS OF MONEY, DAMN IT." To eliminate your limited poverty thinking, you have to discipline your mind to focus on attaining your fantasy financial goals, and master the belief in the power of your mind over financial matters.

Too many people—especially us women people—have a Slave Mentality about money. We feel guilty asking for too much, or for more too soon. Some of this is due to the shackles of our past—maybe our family had only a limited income and we feel bad for earning more than our parents did at the same age. Some of this may stem from society's prejudicial expectations—many of us have been brainwashed to believe that because we're female—or young—we deserve to make less money.

I am hoping that you—yeah YOU out there reading this book—YOU are not operating under this Slave Mentality. Even if you're the youngest person in your department with an office, or the first female ever to make VP in your company, you can't let any feelings of insecurity about being in these positions creep into your attitude. You've got to strut down the hall as if you own the place—and then you probably will.

There's an old Indian proverb, "If you conquer your mind, you conquer the world."

I've said it before, and I'll say it again—this time in a different type face so you'll perk up, take notice—and take it to heart:

The mind is a source of unlimited power. The law of attraction states that whatever you constantly and consistently focus on in your inner world, you will eventually attract in your outer world.

So, if right now you do not have the money—and all the nifty things it can get you that you crave in your life—well, then today is the day to start ordering it all up by mental telephone.

Lori, a Wall Street investor, did just that. Lori kept seeing other investors at her office buying houses, while she still lived in a small Manhattan apartment. So one day she asked herself what amount of money would truly make her happy—allow her the financial freedom to do all the things she wanted to do, buy all the things she wanted to buy, and travel to all the places she wanted to travel. "I wrote this number down on a piece of paper, and put it in my wallet, next to my credit cards for a constant reminder," says Lori. "This number became my mantra, every time I felt defeated, discouraged. I made up my mind that *no matter what*, I was going to earn that money within three years. I then prepared a detailed financial plan so I could visually see the possibility for how it would happen—and then I disciplined myself to stay focused on my plan. It's now three years since I scribbled that fantasy salary down on that paper, and like a psychic who scribbled down a prediction, this salary has come true. I just bought a new house, even, in Sag Harbor"—a posh Long Island community full of bee-you-tiful homes.

I asked her what she thought was her big $64 million tip.

"Discipline your time," said Lori. "Until I made up my mind

I wanted to make that money, I was wasting a lot of my time on non-money-making activities."

Bank on the 80/20 Rule

There's a popular belief that 80 percent of one's results come from 20 percent of one's activities. In sales, for example, it's that top one-fifth of your customers who are driving most of your profits. And, in any occupation, you're often spending 80 percent of your time in routine busy work, while it's your performance in a few critical areas—like attracting new customers or clients—that is the underlying key 20 percent that truly determines your raises and promotions. The trick is to recognize which activities will make the biggest difference in your career, and then focus your energies and attention on these things.

For instance, Phyllis, owner of Phyllis Leibowitz, NYC, a company that imports incredible textiles and decorative home accessories from India, recently found a way to more wisely guard her time. She decided to hire someone else to do her paperwork, recognizing that this is not where her true money-making talents are found. "I realized it would be worth it to pay a small hourly wage to have a bookkeeper, so I could spend more of my time doing what I'm best at—finding interesting products, and dealing one-on-one with store owners."

Paula, a stockbroker, also guards her time by not taking on what she calls "Penny Clients," which is a person with under $5,000 to invest. "I found," explained Paula, "that I spend the same amount of time talking on the phone with someone who has $5,000 as someone who has $5 million, but I make a lot more in commission with the guy—or woman—with $5 million. I decided if I'm going to spend an hour with a client, I want to limit my client base to the folks who I can earn the most commission from. At first this strategy seemed like I was being less productive, because I was less busy, because I had fewer clients. But then this extra time freed me up to seek out a more profitable client base, so in the long run, I am making more money than ever."

You must guard your time like the precious commodity that it is. We all start off each day with same amount. Ted Turner and Madonna each have the same hours in their days as YOU, though it might seem—with what they accomplish—that they have cut a secret deal to increase their daily hour allotment. But the real secret deal they cut is one with themselves—to make sure that their long-term goal is behind every action that they take. They know:

Time is money—

and time wasters are money wasters.

Some of these Time = Money wasters include:

1. Activities that are fun, but no value to your career, like watching Beavis and Butthead during a busy business day (that is, if you're not a TV producer).
2. Activities that seem productive, but are not part of your long-term goal, like going to pointless meetings or staying with a dead-end career or a failing project.
3. Activities that arise out of crisis, such as energy wasters that are created from disorganized planning or goofball management.

Become the Master of Your Mind and Actions and You Will Soon Become the Master of Your Bank Account

You must guard your time assertively—persist and resist being lured away by lesser priorities. When you are finally able to make sure that your every thought and action leads you in the direction of your long-term goal, you will soon find a nice big pot of money waiting for you.

Of course all this takes discipline. But you will find that this discipline leads to more fun, not less. Because the less time you waste on mind-numbing activities that make you hate your job, the more time you have for the fun and challenging parts of your job—and thereby the more energy you'll have to put into your job, and the gobs of cash you'll make that can be be spent on fun, fun, fun.

A trick of the trade is to trick your brain with this trade:

> *You must exchange "painful thoughts of (grumble-grumble) work" with "pleasurable fantasies of (mmm good) indulgences."*

As I stated earlier:

Time = Money.

Which also means:

A careful, aware-ful, wise use of time *now* = A margarita-filled Caribbean vacation, massages, facials, nights out on the town, and other assorted shenanigans *later*.

Once you develop habits to improve your financial destiny, you will be on your way to an improved fun destiny—with a big asterisk attached to that. In fact, picture a really big asterisk right now. I'll help you out, because this is *very* important:

*YOU MUST REMEMBER THIS ABOUT MONEY:

It's *not* everything.

Happiness is not a destination, it is a journey. Of course, it's nice to travel first class on that journey—or the Concorde for that matter! But that doesn't necessarily ensure that you will actually enjoy that journey—after all, on the Concorde you probably don't even have time to watch in-flight movies. Fun and enjoyment come from first attaining an inner satisfaction that you can only reach when you find inner peace and unconditional self-love.

We live in the most affluent culture the world—ever. America has only 6 percent of the world's population, yet we gobble up nearly half the world's natural resources. If material consumption led to happiness, then America would be the happiest nation in the world. But seeing as we are a nation dedicated to Prozacmania, I think that this is not necessarily the case.

Mark, a successful entrepreneurial friend of mine and the President of MBF Capital Corporation, told me he was the happiest in his life when he was first starting to amass his fortune because he was having so much fun. "When I finally made a lot of money," says Mark, "it was cool, exciting, all of that, but my happiest memories will always be about the beginning of my business when I was first discovering who I was, and the challenges I was capable of overcoming." In other words:

Don't wait to make that heap of cash to have heaps of fun.

You must decide RIGHT NOW to be happy. That's *right now*—not to be confused with *a month* from now, *a year* from now, or *$40,000* from now. Make a conscious choice RIGHT NOW to be happy right where you stand (or sit, since most people read sitting down) with the money you have (or have a credit line to have).

Or as Will Rogers warned: "Too many people spend money they haven't earned, to buy things they don't want, to impress people they don't like."

Which reminds me of a story that I told my brother Eric.

My "I Dream of Tricking Genie" Story

If you are ever wandering on a beach and come across a magic bottle, and you by chance rub it, and by chance a *genie comes out and offers to satisfy one of your wishes, there is a trick you can play on this genie to get all your wishes. Now, most people think that this trick is to use your wish to ask the genie for endless wishes. But let's say you have a hip New York genie and she's on to that chicanery by now. Then what? Well, instead of asking for one really big wish, like a mansion, or a Lamborghini, or $1 billion, there is one thing you can ask for that will get you all your other wishes free. And that one thing is: happiness. Because that's really what you're asking for, when you're asking for all those other materialistic things.*

I told this story to my brother and he responded, "Actually Karen, there's something else you can ask for even before happiness—and that's to know who you truly are, so you can find your true happiness."

Today's Fantasy Role-Playing Exercises (and Tips for Cracking Whips)

Bank You Very Much

Before you go in to *ask for a raise,* write up a list of all the *ways you helped raise money* for your company. For instance, did you help snag a big account? Bring in a valuable employee? Increase any profit margins through your creative thinking? If so, be sure to hone in on all this personal value that you brought your company, and not your personal emotional reasons for deserving more cash—like rent increases or car payments.

Save Versus Slave Mentality

A master knows it's good to put money aside. That money in the bank can supply a foundation of courage to quit a job, if needed, or pay for unexpected circumstances. Save 10 percent of everything you make. Do it every time you get a paycheck and it will eventually add up. If you put aside, say, $200 a month for the next 30 years at an annual rate of 7.5 percent, then you will end up with about seven million bucks. Nothing to sneeze at.

Here Comes the Bribe

I f I'm dreading doing a certain project—like writing the next chapter of this book—I bribe myself into it, by promising myself a hedonistic treat when it's completed—like shoes or a dozen roses—or a dozen shoes, if I'm *truly* dreading my work. However, you MUST make sure your project is completed *before* the bribery is received, otherwise you can wind up with some great Italian loafers while you're still loafing around instead of completing your work.

Give Money Some Credit

D o you have subconscious negative views on money that are holding you back from making the bundles your conscious mind thinks it wants? Maybe you feel unworthy indulging in the lifestyle of the rich and anonymous. Or maybe you thought your parents were too money-focused, not love-focused enough—and you're afraid of being the same way. Or you think people with money are superficial or greedy—that there's some truth to that joke: "IF YOU WANT TO KNOW WHAT GOD THINKS OF MONEY LOOK AT SOME OF THE PEOPLE HE GIVES IT TO." Write a list of all the bad things you think about money and the people who earn it. Study your list—and talk yourself out of your ill-will. You should find that once you get more in harmony with receiving money, you'll see money everywhere. Even in the word *harmony*, which will suddenly look to you like *"harmoney."*

What's Your Problem?

*A*lways keep in mind what my friend Adam once told me: "If a problem can be solved by money, it's not a problem." Write a list of your three top problems and disappointments. Are any of these a mere check away from being checked off that list? For instance, are you unhappy with your wardrobe or car? If so, see sentence one of this paragraph.

Spendthrift Shop

*O*ne of the best investments you can make is taking the time to study how you spend your money. For the next few days, write down every lil' thing you spend your money on. Study your list for things you can cut back on, so you can have more money to spend on those things in the list that you just wrote above.

Be a Material Girl

*W*rite down your top ten material goals for this year, the next five years, the next ten years. Figure out how much moola you need to make to afford your desires. Keep your list handy every time you feel lazy about pursuing a work assignment to help inspire you to perspire more—and thereby acquire more.

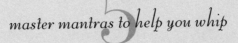

master mantras to help you whip

Your Money Situation

into submission

Next time you feel like your current currency is going against the current of your spending, remember:

1. I am not a SLAVE who gets lured away by lesser priorities. I am a MASTER who keeps my mind and actions centered on my financial goals.

3. I am not a SLAVE who doesn't save. I am a MASTER who puts my money away for a rainy day so I can spend that rainy day on a tropical beach sipping margaritas.

3. I am not a SLAVE who wimpily wastes my time. I am a MASTER who assertively controls my time.

4. I am not a SLAVE who values money over everything. I am a MASTER who has values so I know money is not everything.

5. I am not a SLAVE who hears "no" to a promotion. I am a MASTER who knows to look elsewhere.

Whip

Delegation

Into Submission

or

....

A Pack of Puppies Led by a Pitbull Will Always Be Feared More Than a Pack of Pitbulls Led by a Puppy

....

I attained my very first leadership career position at age twelve. In other words, I was a babysitter. I recognized, even at that young age, a big secret to becoming a Master Delegator, which was basically: *A little subliminal manipulation goes further than big threats.*

For instance, I had a trick for getting the tykes into bed swiftly. Rather than insist, "Okay, put away those matches and knives you're playing with. You gotta go to bed now." I'd say: "Okay, do you want to sleep with the lights on or off?" Inevitably the kids would answer "Off!" and hop into bed.

My Subliminal Delegation Strategy worked for two reasons:

1. I created an *a priori* acceptance that you are indeed doing what I SAY—going to bed NOW—without leaving room to question my authority.
2. I gave the kids a feeling of control over their actions—however, meanwhile, I was still the master behind the master act: Bedtime for Little Bonzoettes.

Later I used this same technique in my post-babysitting leadership career as an ad creative director who needed to lead creative teams into the Clio-winning trenches. For instance, I'd say:

"Do you want to submit your dog food print ad on Tuesday *before* lunch or *after* lunch?"

Either answer would ensure they'd be working under my deadline.

Time after time in the ad biz I found that a Subliminal Delegation Strategy motivates more successfully than an outright spanking and scolding.

You Don't Need to Rule with Sadism— You Can Rule With Gladism

There's always a way you can make people *glad* to do what they have to do. A true master leader can put forth a commanding presence and still be a sweetie-poo-pie—even when employees get downright colicky and uprighteously misbehave. It's important to remember that no matter how mad you may get at unruly employees who refuse to follow the rules of your domain, you must ALWAYS RESIST CRUELLY SPANKING THEIR LITTLE BOTTOMS AND SCOLDING THEM LOUDLY: "Okay, little office boy. You made a mess. Down on your knees." You must especially avoid Public Humiliations. They will only lead to your staff plotting a coup against you.

As a Master Leader, You Must Always Treat People as if Respect Were Contagious— Because It Is

*T*he more you treat people with dignity, the more you will receive respect back. Consider the example of Gandhi, a master disciplinarian who ruled an empire with nothing but tender toughness and a loincloth. Think about it. Here was a frail whippersnapper of a man who managed to whip millions into submission—not by force, not by threats, *but by gentle guidance and an inspiring example.*

My editor, Suzanne, also follows Gandhi's lead in leadership. Except she doesn't opt for the loincloth dress code. Suzanne has been motivating me to finish this very book by being enthusiastic about what I've handed in thus far—and living up to her promises of getting me needed materials on time as well as reconsidering different book cover options I'd asked about.

Suzanne is leading me by example.

Plus, Suzanne also knows when to have Ann, her charming—and funny—assistant, contact me about the little day-to-day activities. Suzanne recognizes that good delegation skills can save a gal from performing that slavish nurturer role all too many women suffer from. Too many women feel like they must do too many things all by themselves.

Pshaw.

You must not be afraid to let go and have someone else do the legwork while freeing you up to get your hands on the work where your true skills can truly show.

After all, when you aren't 100 percent confident in your rights to delegate, you miss out on the benefits of that 80/20 rule I mentioned earlier—that 80 PERCENT OF YOUR POSITIVE RESULTS COME FROM ONLY 20 PERCENT OF YOUR ACTIONS. In other words, you have to know *how* and *when* to delegate some of that spare 80 percent activity you have lying around your desk.

You have to stop feeling guilty about claiming your leader-ship rights over your assistants or your department—or even just that one intimidating employee. You have to stop worrying: "If I'm tough and authoritative and give orders and wield my full power, what will they think? Will they still like me?"—because I have some good news for you about what "they" will think. You ready?

I Am "They"

$\mathcal{Y}$es, this is one of my (many) secret identities, being the fa-mous, anonymous "they." So, next time you feel yourself wondering "What will THEY think if I give orders on what to do and not do?"—well, you must know that, speaking as "they," I'll respect you for believing in your role as a leader.

And others around you will respect you, too, because basi-cally the people you really want respect from anyway are the people who will respect you for being tough, because it shows you're not a spineless wormlike creature.

But—as always—there is one catch:

You have to believe your own hype.

Underneath your firm delegation, must be a firm backbone of belief in your right to wield your power. You must KNOW: "I am meant to be a leader. I am the alpha dog in charge." If you do not fully feel alpha-esque in every nook and cranny of your being, others in your pack will sniff it out on you, and the orders you bark out will not have the necessary bite needed to inspire a following.

For instance, consider that leader in the loincloth. (No, not Suzanne. She's the one in Armani.) I'm talking Gandhi again, folks. Because Gandhi was 110 percent confident in what he was leading his nation toward, a mere soft-spoken word from him reverberated loudly.

Same goes for Michele, a senior editor at *Marie Claire.* She doesn't just tell her freelance writers and staff to do more work because she's into the pleasure of watching people sulk gloomily and simmer with building rage. No, Michele believes in the integrity of the work she is making the effort to produce for her publication, and she inspires the respect of those around because they know she will lead them to produce impressive pieces because she knows what she is doing. Luckily for Michele's team of freelance writers and staff, she also recognizes the following Master Mentality truth:

It's not enough for a leader to believe in herself.
A leader must believe in those she is leading.

Michele knows when to let go. She shows her trust in the talents of those she leads by giving them the power to do their jobs confidently without her every nod of approval.

Same goes with Lois, a senior account executive. "I like to hire people who I know can someday replace me. I don't see this potential as something to make me insecure, I see this as an opportunity for me to eventually rise up and learn my boss's job so I can eventually have his position."

A Great Leader Is Not the One With the Most Slavish Followers, But the One Who Can Create the Most New Master Leaders

Alex, president/part-owner of Charlex, a successful Manhattan editing facility, also recognizes that the knack of perceiving ability in others is an important trait for a master delegator to develop. "I used to get off on being an Emperor, now I get off on being an Empowerer," says Alex. "I truly love to give people power, watch them grow. My whole business has benefited in the process. It all starts when I hire someone. I look for someone who I hope will in many ways be more smart and talented than me, so I know my business will be greater than what I alone could achieve."

Today's Fantasy Role-Playing Exercises
(and Tips for Cracking Whips)

The High Pro-Team Diet

*W*atch your people interactions closely today. Are you the type of person who always sounds as if someone has gotten you out of the shower? Or are you a good cheerleader to the people around you who are working hard? Today decide to SPEAK FLUENT POSITIVESE to everyone you meet. Be enthusiastic and encouraging. Find out what motivates those around you, and jumpstart your staff's "self-motivated" mechanism. You must recognize not everyone wants the same thing. Some people are motivated by money. Some simply want compliments. Some want attention. Some want awards. Some want a nice office. Some want more free time. Today listen closely to what excites people on an individual basis, and decide from now on to keep the promise of this reward burning in the front burner of their minds as they do their jobs.

If You Want to Be the Master of Others, You Must First Be the Master of Yourself

*G*andhi was a tremendous master of self-mastery. He built up his mental toughness to Olympic levels. It paid off big time. The success he experienced in his ability to *control himself in-*

ternally eventually manifested *externally* in the success he experienced in his ability to *lead an entire nation.* Today study your actions to make sure they live up to your words. For instance, are you always late for meetings? Do you supply material in an orderly way to your staff? If not, decide today that you will firmly lead yourself in a way that sets a good example.

Choose or Lose

What qualities do you have that you feel prevent you from thinking of yourself as a master delegator? For instance, do you feel you're not smart enough or talented enough? Or do you get intimidated too quickly by someone who disagrees with your opinions? Do you care too much what others think, and thereby aren't confident enough to stay true to your opinions and commands? Choose today to unshackle any limiting feelings and start believing in yourself. Remember: SELF-RESPECT LEADS TO EMPLOYEE RESPECT. (And having balls eventually leads to having everyone else's balls, too.)

Who Was That Masked Man?

Superman. The Lone Ranger. Catwoman. They all recognized THE POWER OF MAINTAINING MYSTERY IF YOU WANT TO MAINTAIN MASTERY. The more one keeps one's private life private, the more public power one can wield. We've all seen the proof of this—of what happens to presidential hopefuls who become media bait. As soon as there's a *National Enquirer* leakage, a power failure occurs. As a master delegator you want to maintain your *mystery*, not give away your *history*. Not everyone needs to hear the blow-by-blow of the affair you're having with your hunky masseur, or about how you embarrassed yourself in front of a client by misquoting important research data. And be on guard that others are not sharing your history behind your back, either. Keep an ear open for Et Tu Brute brutish gossip, and snip any bad gossip in the bud today.

Mmmmm. The Sweet Smell of Success— and Taste and Sound of It

*P*sychologists acknowledge that the more senses you rile up in folks, the more you can get them to lose their senses, and get caught up in the passion of what you're pitching them. For instance, if you're an architect, it would be wise to boldly display an illustration of your finished job site so your staff will keep in mind what all the huffing and puffing to build this house is about. Or if you're promising your staff a trip to France for work well done, supply croissants or play a little Edith Piaf at your next meeting.

Name Calling

*D*o you know everyone's name who works for you—and even the names of those who work for the people who work for you? Dale Carnegie, author of *How to Win Friends and Influence People*, recognizes that a person's favorite sound to hear is the sound of his name. Decide today to learn the names of five new people at your company. Also, be sure when you're talking to people today that you are using their proper name.

master mantras to help you whip

Delegation

into submission

Next time you want to negate your power to delegate, remember:

1. I am not a SLAVE who allows others to put me into disrespectful bondage. I am a MASTER who knows how to bond with bosses and get work respectfully done.

2. I am not a SLAVE who gives people enough rope so later they can tie me up with it. I am a MASTER who establishes good ties with people so we can get projects done together.

3. I am not a SLAVE who delegates through image, but without masterhood of self. I am a MASTER of myself first, and then, by example, I become a master leader.

4. I am not a SLAVE who seeks out sadism as a way of life. I am a MASTER who recognizes gladism is a better motivational methodology.

5. I am not a SLAVE who raises my fist fiercely. I am a MASTER who puts my fist down—but gently.

Heavy Breather

Day

or

What a Difference Two Weeks Can Make

Good morning. And it's going to be a darn good morning for you today, because I'm giving you the day off.

No, no. This does *not* mean that you get to call in sick to work, and lounge around in your Smurf pajamas eating bonbons and watching Ricki Lake. No, it's off with the Smurf PJs and into the office you go.

What I mean instead is that today you will not be learning anything new in this book. Instead, you will be taking a breather and learning what's new *outside this book*—in your career life.

It's (Yikes) Weigh-in Time

....

*Y*ou know how in diets you get on a scale after a certain period of time to see what kind of progress you've made? Well, Mistress Karen wants you to get on a scale—of one to ten—RIGHT NOW—and rate how you've been doing at whipping yourself and your career and your tush into shape in the following ways:

1. Level of day-to-day change in my behavior when it comes to each daily subject Mistress Karen has covered.
2. Level of long-term change in my career progression when it comes to each daily subject Mistress Karen has covered (in other words, have these lessons helped me move closer to my goal?).
3. Level of how others have noticed a change in me when it comes to each daily subject Mistress Karen has covered.
4. Level of how my overall confidence in pursuing my career goal has changed thanks to Mistress Karen.

Okay?
Ready?

Once again, these are the subjects you must objectively rate:

MISDIRECTION	BLAME
FEAR	IMPATIENCE
CYNICISM	PROCRASTINATION
REGRET	LISTENING
ANGER	HEALTH
WORRY	EARNINGS
MOOD	DELEGATION

NOW . . . today while you're at the office be alert to how expertly you whip these 14 subjects into submission, and rate your efforts on a scale of one to ten (ten being a whipping success, one being a wimpy effort).

Watch yourself all day today: Are you listening to your assistant when she clearly needs your help or guidance? Or are you becoming a wee bit testy? Are you stressed out about a project and so you decide to blow off eating your midday meal? Or are you calmly taking a break from a work crisis with a leisurely lunch—away from your desk? You get the idea.

LATER . . . at the end of the day, Mistress Karen wants you to get back on the scale and weigh in once again.

THEN, LATER LATER . . . if you feel Mistress Karen would be happy with your progress—THEN AND ONLY THEN—can you put on those Smurf PJs, and get out those bonbons.

Good luck.

Whip

Perfectionism

Into Submission

or

Hey, We All Forget to Floss on Occasion

I n my last book I mentioned a Bazooka Joe comic that I'd again like to share.

Picture this: Bazooka Joe is talking to a painter who says: "I don't get it. I paint and I paint and I paint. And not only isn't my painting getting any better, my painting is getting worse."

Bazooka Joe responds: "Actually, it's not that your painting is getting worse. It's that your taste is getting better."

That tiny comic speaks volumes to me.

I've been writing my second novel, *Cleavage,* for the last three years, and I keep getting more and more aware of how I want to perfect it—and thereby further and further away from ever finishing it. It seems every paragraph I write needs a little bit of finessing, reworking, reediting, or just generally needs to be nuked out of existence.

In other words I'm having a wee bit of a problem with perfectionism.

Basically what my perfectionism is about is FEAR—one of those aforementioned separated-at-birth fears:

1. Fear of success.
2. Fear of failure.

Like many people who won't finish up the last 10 percent of a project, I'm not sure which category the fear of completing my novel falls under.

All throughout my life, I've always been an active perfectionist. (Remember: I'm the one who told my psychic that "I'm not nearly perfectionistic enough.") Even when things are going really really well for me, I can always find something to key in on that could be better. I could win the Nobel Peace Prize, fly to Sweden, start getting dressed for my award ceremony, and I'd look in the mirror and say: "Damn, if only I were five pounds thinner."

But I am trying to break my perfectionism mania. I repeatedly remind myself to remember Reinhold Weibehur's prayer:

"Please God, give me the serenity to accept the things I cannot change, the courage to change the things I can, and the wisdom to know the difference. Oh, and let my dry cleaning be ready as promised on Tuesday."

The prayer goes something like that.

Damn. How could I not remember that prayer exactly?

I hate not being perfect.

Actually, let's take a look at that above prayer, shall we? It basically sums up the two different forms of perfectionism:

1. Bad, futile exasperating perfectionism—the kind that requires "the serenity to accept the things you can't change."

2. Good, helpful, inspiring perfectionism—the kind that requires "the courage to change the things you can."

It's up to you to build up your wisdom muscles so you can tell the two apart.

If a project you are working on right now falls under the second, "courage-required" category then plow forward. For instance, say your boss is expecting your first marketing report and the topic is why you feel your company should expand its operations regionally, and in your report you disagree with something your boss said in a meeting—and you feel you didn't go into enough detail supporting your point in your report. Face your fears head on and go for it: Add the extra info. And for extra courage to add that extra effort, it might help to remind yourself of:

1. A famous little Zen ditty: "An expert was once a beginner, too." Go for it.
2. Something my buddy Steve once said: "The more you're willing to risk failure, the more you probably want something."

HOWEVER . . . you must learn to relax if a project that you are trying to perfect right now falls under the first "serenity-required" category—for instance, you already handed the report in and your boss took it with him on his plane trip to Hong Kong—you must force your mind—through conscious awareness—to de-focus away from your unfixable circumstance and refocus instead on:

1. Your long-term goals.
2. Your fabulous talent.
3. What you have in your life right now that you should appreciate.

Basically, you should always keep in mind what Colette, the writer, once said: "What a wonderful life I've had. I only wish I'd realized it sooner."

Or you can keep in mind what Susan, the junior lawyer, once said, "Every day I remind myself I'm working as fast as I can. I know I'm not a partner yet in the firm, but I also know I'm a hard worker—and further ahead in my career than a lot of my peers. I know I'm still single and not married—but I'm still youthful and having fun—most of the time—dating."

We women in particular have a tough time with perfectionism. Society has given us a larger checklist than men of things to obsess about improving in our lives. A woman's under pressure to be a respected professional, beauty queen, sex maven, therapist surrogate to friends, aerobics star, and cookie-baking mom.

The result?

Too many of us wind up being preoccupied with what's missing in our lives, rather than what we have.

The result?

Some of us see our career glass of water as half-full, others as half-empty—and still others see it as goddamn career water and not La Career Dom Perignon.

For those of you who fall under this last category, here's your new mantra: *"Me? I'm not perfect, but I'm doing the best I can. Me? I'm not perfect, but I'm doing the best I can. Me? I'm not perfect, but I'm doing the best I can."*

I try to repeat this mantra to myself daily. My goal is to actually believe the following:

People will value me even if I am only near perfect.

I know, I know—I *know*. There are qualities in a person that are even more important than achieving perfection. In particular an important quality to look for in another is the ability to have a strong enough character to keep on going even through mistakes and screw-ups. In other words:

Persistence is waaay more important than perfection.

Successful business people know that success is more about how you do over time than how you do each and every time. It's all a numbers game. In fact, there's a saying: "If you want to succeed twice as fast, double your failure ratio."

Risky Business

Consider the successful career of Babe Ruth. He was not only one of the highest hitters of home runs, but also one of the highest striker-outers. What we babes must learn from that Babe is that our career quest should not be about perfection but about how often we're stepping up to the plate full-force. You've got to take a big ol' whack at the ball in order to hit the Big One.

Or look at Thomas Edison. He admits that he tried unsuccessfully over 10,000 times to invent the lightbulb. However, each and every time he didn't let perfectionism block his determination. He told himself, "I didn't fail. I just discovered another way *not* to invent the electric lightbulb."

Tommy, a furniture designer, encouraged himself in the same way as Edison. It took him six months longer than he had anticipated to design a portable lightweight chair. But he finally did. And now he has orders lined up from big department stores across the country.

You are always going to make mistakes. The trick is to learn, learn, learn. Each mess-up always teaches us something. As Nietzsche says: "What doesn't kill you makes you really cranky—I mean stronger."

Damn. Why didn't I remember that quote exactly?

I hate not being perfect.

Anyway . . . You have a choice:

1. You can choose not to learn from mistakes, revel in your misery, and not move ahead.

2. You can choose not to risk making a mistake in the first place, and move behind. At best you'll be hitting singles all your life—batting in low-glory, low-profile events, while others around you are stealing home plate.

3. You can choose to risk making every and all kind of mistakes in your pursuit of career happiness, and know any and every which way—win or lose—you will be moving ahead, because you'll be either earning more or learning more.

Today's Fantasy Role-Playing Exercises
(and Tips for Cracking Whips)

Give Yourself a 15 Percent Screw-up Factor

*N*obody's perfect. We all screw up. Decide today to allow yourself a 15 percent screw-up ratio on any project you are doing at your office. This includes typose.

The Only Thing Worse Than Not Being Perfect Is Somebody Else Not Being Perfect

*H*ave you been particularly hard on others at the office who aren't performing 100 percent perfectly? If so, recognize that when someone makes a mistake, it doesn't always mean he didn't try hard enough. Today decide to give the people around you the benefit of a doubt that they are doing the best they can—and the benefit of your 15 percent Screw-up Factor.

If Only You Could Break the "if Only" Habit

What "if onlys" do you have in your life that are keeping you from moving forward? For instance, "if only" I had more time to get a resume together and interview, I'd get a better job. Or "if only" I made more money I'd move into a better apartment. Study your "if only" list. Decide today to break one of your "if only" habits by following the following:

1. Know thyself—know what you want.
2. Make a plan, and go for it.
3. A month from now, analyze your results thus far—without judgment over what went wrong.
4. Adapt according to what you've learned. Try another plan, but keep your same goal.

Lose Ego. Win Everything

So you screwed up. Everybody screws up. Well, not everybody. Some people get it done right. Ask them how they manage to do it. Make a lunch date with someone who has succeeded at a job you've failed at. Ask him to advise you.

Do a Little Hula of Joy

Forget about what's wrong in your career life for a moment. Write a list of everything you need to appreciate that you have brought to you. Not bad, eh?

master mantras to help you whip

Perfectionism

into submission

Next time you feel perfectionism perking up inside you, remember:

1. I am not a SLAVE who says, "If I don't do this right I'll die." I am a MASTER who says, "We all die anyway. It won't kill me to keep in mind that I am trying to get this done as best I can, and that's enough."

2. I am not a SLAVE who finds myself breathing down my own back to perform perfectly. I am a MASTER who breathes easily about performing well.

3. I am not a SLAVE who says, "I fucked up and now I am doomed to failure." I am a MASTER who says, "One bad screw-up don't spoil the whole bunch of successes ahead of me."

4. I am not a SLAVE who finds misery in my mistakes. I am a MASTER who seeks mastery of my problems after a mistake.

5. I am not a SLAVE who is a whiner about what went wrong. I am a MASTER who is a winner and moves on and on.

Whip *Meaninglessness* *Into Submission*

or

....

Is It Worth It to Suck Up to God?

....

I often wonder whether there is a divine order hidden within all the chaos of life—if indeed nothing in this universe is random—and both form and formlessness are interconnected within the same vibrating field.

In other words, why the heck does my computer keep crashing?

I JUST DON'T GET IT.

What is God trying to tell me? Whoever is in charge up there seems to have tremendous mood shifts—fluctuating without warning from generous to sadistic. Perhaps God is a woman with PMS. Or perhaps I'm misinterpreting God. Perhaps God is a benevolent being, and each time my computer crashes, it's just his or her way of saying: Hey, take the day off.

Actually, I don't mean to start ranking on God. In fact, I

consider myself a very religious person. For a girl who's written a book with the word *penis* in the title, many of you out there would be surprised by how strongly religion has influenced me and guided me through all the adversity in my career life. And I've had some real major heartbreaks and disappointments—quite a few jobs that I didn't get that I majorly wanted. Plus, quite a few jobs I *did* get that afterward I wished I hadn't majorly wanted. Not to mention all my numerous computer crashes—about three—the hard drive and all. (You know how there was Typhoid Mary? I consider myself Technology Mary. I get near any piece of technology, and it's doomed to die.)

My career life has been a rocky, rocky road. In fact, I've often joked that the title of my career memoirs will be *What Was I Thinking?* (And the title of my dating memoirs will be *Don't Get Me Started . . .* but don't get me started with that either.)

ANYWAY . . . my point?

Being a Master of Your Destiny Requires First and Foremost Becoming a Master Interpreter of All the Bad Shit That (Inevitably) Happens

*B*asically, the way I see religion is this: It's less about prayers and is-there-a-God-or-isn't-there?, and *more* about a way of viewing and interpreting the world. I recognize after all these 27 years of my life (yes, I'm lying about my age; that's one of the treasured secrets I keep between me and God)— anyway, I recognize that I can't change a lot of what goes on around me, but I can change my view of life so it remains full of meaning and hope.

I want the same for you.

Or to put it yet another way. It's your choice:

1. Commit yourself to the belief that everything has a reason.
2. Get committed.

Trust me. You can go crazy fighting against unexpected calamity, heartbreaking disappointments, and the horror of seeing those $300 boots you just bought on sale for $150—unless you find meaning in your pain. After every bad thing that happens you must learn to pick yourself up by your $300 bootstraps—and other assorted leather wares—and start again with a smarter, feistier, more aware perspective.

A Master of One's Destiny Recognizes That Every Bad Thing That Happens Has a Grander, Hopeful, Inspiring Lesson to Be Learned

*I*n fact, when you finally learn to find the greater meaning in your suffering—when you can finally see adversity as offering a more profound purpose than simply letting you know, "Nyah, nyah, got you, SUCKER!"—you are on your way to a more fulfilling life. Actually all of this leads me to one of my little big secrets for happiness—which I will now generously share.

At Last, the Secret to Happiness:

*R*ationalize, rationalize, rationalize.
    In other words, next time your career careens in the wrong direction, or gives you an unexpected CLUNK in your head/heart/groin, you must stop and figure out how to rationalize that this adversity that you are enduring is God's way to spur you on to greater effort to become a greater person.
    That's what I do.
    For instance, remember that story I told you about how I

was going to develop a TV show with those producers in L.A. who gave me their verbal commitment to a specific amount of money—then backed out? You can be sure, I was majorly bummed. In other words: furious. In other words: I was low on cash at that particular time in my life and worried about paying my mortgage.

"Why, God? Why me?" I kept thinking.

Then I called up my blessed rationalization skills, and could see (thank God—and I mean that "thank God" in every sense of that expression) that this adversity was brought to me to teach me something.

At first I thought that something was: *Boy, am I an idiot.*

But no, that wasn't it.

Well, yes, it was.

But, to be more specific, my lesson was: *I need to be less trusting of people.*

"I keep telling you," said my boyfriend at that time, "you need to assess more."

"Oh," I said, "I thought you said I need to *obsess* more! So I've been doing that."

Just kidding.

I also realized this adversity reminded me:

1. Money is important, but not everything. Your health and those who you love and those who love you are what truly matter in this life.
2. I didn't want to do goofy TV shows anyway. That particular show was to be called "The Sex Files" and was going to be a slightly more cerebral *Ricki Lake*, with me as the host. I needed to remember why I had quit my ad job—to do something more meaningful with my writing skills. This adversity reminded me to stay true to my true career path.

By coincidence—or some divine synchronicty—at that time I kept a journal. I was rereading a portion of it that I had written a month before the L.A. fiasco and saw the following sentence:

"I need to make up my mind to be an author."

ONLY . . . I reread it by mistake as:

"I need to WAKE UP my mind to be an author."

That's when I realized that this wrong reading was actually the *righter phrasing*. This L.A. fiasco was my WAKE-UP CALL to pursue being the author I wanted to be and not get sidetracked from my true goal. I did manage to find the grander purpose in my adversity—to see it as a reminder to stay true to my most important life values.

And that's what adversity can do for all of us: serve as a WAKE-UP CALL to remind us who we really are and what we really value. In fact, this is the actual Sanskrit definition of "Buddhism": "awakening." And this "awakening" is what Buddhism hopes to inspire—and what I hope this book will inspire in YOU.

You have a choice:

> *Adversity can break you— or give you the breakthrough you need to see yourself and your life more clearly.*

I believe being able to persist in the face of adversity is the true measure of your true character. There's an old expression:

"Circumstances don't make the man, they reveal him."

You must live this anew each day.

And you won't be living it alone.

Almost Every Fortune 500 Member Could Also Belong to the Misfortune 500 Club

*H*enry Ford went bankrupt five times before he got his car business rolling. Disney, too, made some Goofy mistakes that almost bankrupted him. Or just look at John Travolta's career. In my last book, I advised people who are on the verge of giving up or breaking down to repeat this soothing mantra: "JOHN TRAVOLTA IS BACK, JOHN TRAVOLTA IS BACK, JOHN TRAVOLTA IS BACK." It works like a charm.

Or you should consider a very recent success case that supports believing in fortune waiting on the other end of misfortune: Laura Day, author of the best-seller *Practical Intuition*—who now has a $3 million book deal for future insightful tomes. (NOTE: See my chapter on intuition for more about this book and this highly cool lady.) Day's career didn't start off so grandly. It was only after going through one of the worst times in her life that she discovered her career-calling. Day had divorced her husband, and then—as if divorce isn't hard enough—eight months later she gave birth to her son, Samson. At that time in her life, she had a pile of bills from her divorce—with more bills to come. She worried about how to pay them and still pay attention to Samson—how to be a good full-time mommy. That's when her intuition really kicked in. She realized she needed to write a book on intuition to get her out of her predicament. It worked. *Voila:* a millionairess and an attentive, involved, full-time mommy was born.

Day says, "At the point when you're most lost, that's when intuition kicks in."

I agree—and also believe that's when your physical prowess reaches a pinnacle and your highest creativity kicks in.

For an example of the first situation, consider United States skater, Todd Eldredge, who inspired *People* magazine to say the following about him: "If they gave out medals for bad breaks, Todd Eldredge would be a lock for the gold." Time and time again, crucial medal-winning opportunities in Eldredge's career kept being delayed by things like a bad back and a fever. Then in October of '97 it happened again. Four months before the Nagano Olympics, misfortune again struck—he partially dislocated his shoulder during warm-up. Eldredge struck back at the fates. Through sheer will and guts, he channeled all his inner resources and miraculously popped his shoulder back in and skated an impressive first-place routine in that competition. He's now pulled his career up to a place where he's eligible to compete for his dream—the gold in the Olympics.

Dick Button, ABC skating analyst, had this to say about him: "Todd is not a quitter, he's a fighter. He's got a single-mindedness that most skaters who fail don't have."

In other words, failure and misfortune didn't damper Eldredge's spirits, they riled his spirits up to a level he might not ever have been able to achieve had he not suffered misfortune in the first place.

Now, for an example of how properly channeled misfortune can help you tap into superior creative highs, consider the success story of Trey Parker and Matt Stone. Both were self-confessed "geeky" guys in high school who went on to become the maniacal creative duo behind Comedy Central's highly successful animated series *South Park*.

Parker begain his career less than auspiciously: He got his butt kicked out of film school for missing too many classes. Then he paired up with Stone and the two started off making goofy films on a goofy budget—like *Cannibal: The Musical* and *Giant Beaver of Southern Sri Lanka*—without much positive feedback. But they plowed on for over seven years, refusing to give up. Soon they went from experimenting with filming peculiar projects like a little girl who's dressed in a beaver costume and creates pandemonium in a town (a "no go"), to doing odd stuff with construction paper. Parker and Stone would sit on the floor of their apartment and cut up colored paper into bizarre, animated characters. This last concept—now known as *South*

Park—not only hit, but hit big, upgrading Comedy Central's ratings and moving over thirty million bucks' worth of merchandise. Their secret? They didn't let rejection lower their spirits and creativity level. They didn't sell out. They took it all as a challenge to see just how far they could go creatively to make an impact—and they did. (I recommend checking out this show—especially if you're undergoing some misfortune right now. It will make you giggle.)

There are infinite stories of good things coming to those who wait—and don't get weighted down. Read *Chicken Soup for the Soul* for more bowls full of examples of these *now* successful people who did not let failure stop them but instead let it propel them forward to become stronger, more inspired—and highly inspiring—successful people.

It's Not the Feat. It's the Emotion

*B*asically, everything that happens in this world only has the meaning you give it with your thoughts—and you are master of your thoughts. It's up to you to see the world and its schizo ups and downs in the best possible light with the best possible attitude. When it comes right down to it, your life is not so much about what you do—at the office or outside the office—it's more about *who you're being while you're doing what you're doing—and having it done to you.*

So who are you?

Are you being true to the you that you see yourself as when you do what you do at your job? Are you being kindhearted, honest, altruistic, good-tempered, attentive to others? Or are you being a real curmudgeon (aka dinkhead) because you're cranky at God and life? And when bad things happen at your job, are you choosing the higher path to become even more inspired to be the best, most successful person you can be—and not some woe-is-me loser who feels sorry for yourself? Are you always looking for the grander meaning in the bad shit? If not, you must start today to tell yourself that everything around you—the bad and the good—is meant to teach you things that can help you evolve into the best you, your most favorite ideal you. If at first you must fake this positive attitude about the world, then fake it. Like all habits, eventually these positive thoughts in time will feel true. *Your act will become fact:*

You must consistently believe in raisons d'etre instead of grapes of wrath.

Viktor Frankl, a psychoanalyst who survived his imprisonment in a concentration camp during the Holocaust, later wrote a classic in the field called *Man's Search for Meaning.* In this book he promotes a therapy called "logotherapy," which is about finding the meaning in one's suffering. Frankl believed that the prisoners who managed to survive the camps were a special breed of people who had made the conscious choice to view the Holocaust as having a grander life purpose for them, that these people felt within that they were meant to survive because they had something important to offer life—and, even more so, that the Holocaust had better prepared them to offer these particular services to the world. Frankl himself believed his calling was to bring "logotherapy" to people everywhere. He survived, and did. His logotherapy treatment is now used by thousands of therapists in the United States to help patients who are undergoing crisis. One of these patients was Lisa, a Wall Street analyst.

Opportunity Practices Its Knocking at the School of Hard Knocks

Seven years ago, Lisa discovered at a routine doctor's exam that she had a lump in her breast. Further investigation revealed she had breast cancer and might die. She underwent three years of chemotherapy that not only saved her life—but forever changed it. She left her Wall Street firm and now works for a national health facility for women in its department of fundraising. "I now feel that my tragedy with breast cancer was meant to be. I have skills as a financial analyst and contacts in the financial world that can be better used to help people like myself who are suffering. My life is richer now. If I had a choice between living as I was—healthy and as a Wall Street analyst— or undergoing the last few years of disease and doing what I'm doing now for sick women across the country, there's no question, I'd choose the latter any day of the week."

Like Lisa, you can make your life a lot happier when you devote yourself to working toward something, when you are able to organize your goals around your values and finding profound meaning in your life. So start today, goddamn it. Or rather, God deems it. Or something like that.

All of this reminds me of a goofy—yet not too far from philosophical—cartoon I recently saw of one hand puppet talking to another hand puppet.

"I don't know," the one says to the other, "sometimes I question whether there really is a hand."

In other words, it's like this:

You must not only have faith that there is "a hand"—you must have faith that *you have a hand* in being who you want to be in this lifetime.

Today's Fantasy Role-Playing Exercises
(and Tips for Cracking Whips)

You Are Eligible to Register for a Karma Credit Card

*T*oday you must make a commitment to pursue something bigger than yourself. You don't have to leave your job to do this. You can find worthy ideals in serving a charity or visiting an old-age home. What do you believe needs fixing in this world? Decide today that you will make a valuable contribution in helping to get it fixed. You'll be paid back not with money but with the biggest payback of all: a grander sense of yourself and your grander life purpose.

Reedit That Movie-for-One Called *Your Career Life*

*P*retend you are a Hollywood screenwriter, and find the meaning in your career suffering. First, study act one and "return to the scene of your career crime." Recognize all the grumble-*grumble*-GRUMBLE bad things that have happened. Now study act two and "return to the scene of the sublime." See yourself as a fictional movie character and see what lesson this character was meant to learn at the climax of the story—thereby giving you the ultimate release of a climax of joy in your life— your act three. Now write your act three—show how this fictional character has evolved since act one.

Shut Up and Meditate

*Y*ou must get addicted to the habit of relaxing more when misfortune strikes, and thereby being better able to stay calm and confident and focused on attaining your goals. After all, one bad day or report or job loss doesn't spoil the whole bunch in your grand scheme of 80 years of life.

master mantras to help you whip

Meaninglessness

into submission

Next time you start getting cranky at God, get thankful, instead, and remember:

1. I am not a SLAVE who finds misery at my company. I am a MASTER who seeks mastery over adversity.

2. I am not a SLAVE feels powerless over my problems. I am a MASTER who feels powerful after problems.

3. I am not a SLAVE who sees torturers. I am a MASTER who sees teachers.

4. I am not a SLAVE who says, "shmucky, shmucky me" after a setback. I am a MASTER who says "lucky, lucky me"—then finds out what that lucky thing is about.

5. I am not a SLAVE who sees a boulder in my path. I am a MASTER who sees a bolder path.

Whip

Communication

Into Submission

or

....

Saying Difficult Things Is Better
Than Fixing Difficult Problems

....

I never fake having an orgasm.

Though I have faked *not* having had an orgasm—so the guy keeps going and going . . . and going. And thereby—hopefully—neither of us will know if we're coming or going.

But I remain adamant about never faking the orgasm itself. I feel in the long run everyone loses. Me first—on my end, so to speak. And the guy, too. After all, if he doesn't learn what he can do to please a woman, he will repeat his errors not only with me, but with future women once I potentially break up with him due to lack of connection and subconscious resentment.

Faking orgasm in bed has a lot in common with bad communication in business. After all:

It's better to communicate difficult stuff sooner,
or communication will get more difficult later.

For example, consider Nana, a film editor. She was editing a short film with a writer/director who wasn't paying her much, but promised her that the short film would play the festivals and help Nana's career. Nana kept thinking up editing ideas for how to improve the the film, but felt too intimidated to stand her ground about them. In the end, Nana was left with a piece of work she didn't feel proud about—and was thereby of no value to her career. On top of this, Nana also felt resentment because she didn't get paid more money—though Nana never spoke up to ask for more money.

Janis, a psychologist I know, has an expression she tells her patients who are having trouble communicating, "Say what you mean and mean what you say."

It's always important to say what you feel out loud—even if you think it sounds goofy, because it will prevent goofy grievances further down the line. Plus, people will respect you for speaking up and being sincere about how you feel. In fact, I've found being sincere to be a very manipulative method to get what you want. Just kidding. Sort of.

My point: Time and time again, more and more scientific proof comes in each day that shows that as surely as $e = mc^2$:

The quality of your communication =
The quality of your career.

What you *don't* ask for is what you *don't* get. Although you may feel you work with some people who are from another planet, unfortunately they are usually not of the Vulcan breed who can read your mind. If you want to be heard and understood, you've got to speak up, girlfriend!

Though I admit, even *I*—the girl with the word *penis* in my book title—have experienced my share of problems communicating.

For instance, recently I was in a Chinese restaurant and asked my waiter if he had a telephone. He nodded enthusiastically and said, "Yes, yes. I bring to you right now." I was impressed. Chung was quite the dude, spoiling me with this special telephone service. Next thing I knew he had plopped a plate of noodles in front of me. "What's this?" I asked, confused. "Chow fun," he said, equally confused. "You said you wanted chow fun."

My point? Hmmm . . . I know I had one. Oh, yeah: Invest in a cellular and when using it remember: It's not only *what* you say, but *how* you say it. Don't slur. Be clear. Be loud. Be aware of your precision in language. Try not to enter into the Fluff Zone of hazy, lazy word choice. Most specifically, be specific.

And now to demonstrate how to communicate more specifically, I will communicate specifically *how*—while using a sophomoric sex joke.

Mistress Karen's Seven Tips To Improve Your Oral Technique

(ahem, that was it—my aforementioned sophomoric sex joke)

1. Decide first what you specifically need to say or ask for.
2. Ask for it with a focused belief. If you're not convinced about the rightness of what you're asking for, the other person won't be, either.
3. Explain clearly *why* you need what you need. Get them feeling involved.
4. Make sure you are asking someone who can truly help you—someone who has the right resources and expertise—and whose resources and expertise are matched by sympathy and availability.
5. Create value for the person you're asking something from—explain how you can you help him, too.

6. Ask until you get what you want, perhaps readjusting how you ask, until you ultimately do get it.

7. Thank the person.

Okay, so let's say you follow Mistress Karen's Improved Oral Technique, and still you feel misunderstood and powerless. What next?

Maybe it's not your mind but your body that needs work. In other words, *maybe your body language is speaking louder than your words.* Perhaps you were slumped in your chair, so your posture gave off no command behind your commands. Or you avoided eye contact, so your sense of "I" behind your "I want" felt less solid and more resistible.

Or maybe it's not "what" you said but "the wear" behind it. Perhaps your wardrobe warred with your words. For instance, were you wearing a very short skirt and therefore was the medium of your message shortshrifted by the message of sexuality? Or the miscommunication that anyone who dresses in a nonbusiness way is someone not to do business with?

Another consideration: You were having one of those Men Are from Mars, Women Are from Brooklyn kinda things. I believe we are called the opposite sex for good reason. We are very opposite. Some of this is displayed in how differently we communicate. Primarily, men see conversation as "informing" talk—an opportunity to see how to fix something. Women see it as "informal talk"—an opportunity to bond. Plus there are a plethora of other differences. Check out not only John Gray's book *Men Are from Mars, Women Are from Venus*, but also Deborah Tannen's book *Talking 9 to 5*. Both will help you speak fluent Martian and fluent Venusian.

Lastly, you should consider whether you were, as they say, "looking for oranges in the hardware store." Meaning? Maybe the person you were attempting to communicate with did not have the goods to deliver—either emotionally, intellectually, materially, or authoritatively. If that's so, move on. Go elsewhere.

Okay, now let's say you said something to someone that irked him in some way—or else someone else said something irksome and jerksome to you. There is now permanent static in the communication signals being sent back and forth between you two. When you walk into the ladies' room, she walks briskly out. When you're at a meeting, he doesn't address you—or worse, he speaks derogatorily to you. *What now?*

Nine Ways to Solder a Communication Gap With a Colleague

1. Do not speak from anger. Wait. But don't carry the weight for too long.
2. You need not only the right time to talk, but the right place. Pick a setting you feel is conducive to open, honest communication (like an empty office late at night where no one will interrupt you, and not the Baby Doll Go-Go Club).
3. State up front that your goal is to build the relationship back up, not rip it down. Keep this end goal in mind as you talk.
4. Agree not to interrupt each other until you're each done explaining your POV.
5. When explaining your feelings, be careful not to insult the other person's character, but instead talk about the miscommunication/misbehavior/whatever it is that you're pissed off about—as if it were a separate entity outside this person, an entity that can be studied objectively and then lopped off.
6. Now, state the basics of your grievance—then shut up. Before you go rambling on and on, ask this other dinkhead—I mean, business person—to explain why he did what he did—and this is the hard part—you

must *actually* listen *openly*. Be sure you are not projecting your own inner turmoil onto him—you know, seeing life through dysfunctional childhood glasses.

7. Make your rebuttal to his defense short and tout-de-suite.

8. Ask what the other person thinks the two of you can do *together* to be sure to get to the root of your mutual grievance. Then *together* figure out how to pull out the roots of this grievance so it will not grow back.

9. End on a good note, maybe even complimenting this now recovered dinkhead for being open—or find some other quality that reinforces the positive bond you now—God willing—share.

Okay, That's It for the Oral Test. Now Let's Do the Written

Sometimes it doesn't pay to talk. It pays to e-mail.
    Or fax.
Or send a memo.
You can say the more difficult stuff more easily on the written page. For instance, if you want to ask for more money, but have trouble talking money, type it up and e-mail it out.

Today's Fantasy Role-Playing Exercises
(and Tips for Cracking Whips)

Just Like, Only Different

If you don't own a dictionary or a thesaurus, get one and keep it handy. Browse through it when writing reports, or even on a coffee break, shopping for the newer, righter, more rectified (look it up) words.

Are You Miss Communication—
or Miscommunicating?

Is there someone at your office that you feel you've been having underlying tension or miscommunication with? If so, today invite him out for a cup of mochaccino and empathy. Talk it out.

That Space Between Words

Sometimes what you don't say shouts very loudly. For instance, are you behind in returning phone calls? If so, you could be sending a message to someone you don't mean to send, like you are not important enough, or I am not professional enough. Today call back anybody you owe a call.

Also . . . another seemingly silent but loud communication to keep in mind is *where you call from.* For instance, whenever I was at MTV—even merely dropping off work I'd completed—

I'd use their phones to call other clients (like Comedy Central, E!, L'Oreal, Revlon, etc.). My goal? By calling from MTV, I knew I was keeping up my image of being busy and wanted. It worked. Often prospective clients would say "Can I call you back?" I'd say, "Uh, no I'm at MTV right now. I'm hard to reach." My client base doubled using this strategy.

Speaking Fluent Subtitles

*P*ick one person today—it can be your boss, an employee, a colleague—and decide to listen extra hard to this person's body language and subtext. What new thing did you learn about him?

master mantras to help you whip

5

Communication

into submission

Next time you feel you're tripping over your tongue, bite the bullet and remember:

1. I am not a SLAVE who gets off on beating around the bush. I am a MASTER who goes out on a limb to say what I mean.

2. I am not a SLAVE who enjoys complaining about being ignored. I am a MASTER who delights in speaking up.

3. I am not a SLAVE who restrains myself from full expression. I am a MASTER who retrains myself to free expression.

4. I am not a SLAVE who suffers the pain of being held back from saying what I want to say. I am a MASTER who gets off on being in total control of what I say.

5. I am not a SLAVE who sits in meetings with a gag in my mouth. I am a MASTER who spits out what I have to say in a timely fashion.

Whip

Guilt

Into Submission

or

....

Stop Playing Keeping Down with the Joneses

....

I have a confession. I sometimes have a hard time telling men what I do for a living. And that's not just because it involves using the word *penis* in my job description. It's because I sometimes feel embarrassed by my success—especially if I'm more successful than the man sitting across the fettucini alfredo, trying to woo me with wit and charm (and a lot of vino).

I remember after I got my Miramax deal, I was dating this still-life photographer who was having trouble with his career, and I felt guilty that mine was taking off so smoothly. I know that I am not alone. Many women I know (OK, me included) not only allow ourselves to feel bad about doing better than men, but for surpassing our women friends, as well. I call this "Keeping Down With the Joneses" Syndrome. Though it's your standard Garden Variety Guilt Syndrome—and it starts growing in childhood.

Homegrown Guilt

As little girls, we feel punished if we stand out. We're called bossy when we speak our minds or we're told we're showing off when we know all the answers. Many of us then carry this emotional baggage into adulthood with us and unpack it at the office—or at a candlelit dinner with a man we fancy (aka wanna shag). We worry if we do too well in our jobs, we risk losing intimacy. Many of us experience subconscious vertigo about rising too high—so we hold ourselves back, keep ourselves down.

Which reminds me of a lil' Buddhist tale:

The Elephant Truly NEVER Forgets

The first trick an elephant trainer trains an elephant to do is not to escape. When the elephant is still but a baby, the trainer chains the infant's leg to a huge log, so when/if the elephant tries to escape, the log proves stronger, and it gives up. Eventually the elephant becomes so used to its captivity that even when it has grown huge and strong, all the trainer has to do is tie the chain around the elephant's leg to anything—even a tiny little twig—and the elephant won't even try to escape. It has become a prisoner of its past.

Guilting the Lily

We are constantly fighting a similar battle against our past—restraints that may or may not really exist but that nevertheless bind us with guilt about going for those gobs of cash or that plethora of power. It's just as important for us women to learn to feel okay about indulging in these kinds of goodies, as with food and sex.

In his book *The Pursuit of Pleasure*, Lionel Tiger explains: "Pleasure and its availability loom as a resource, a lot like wealth. And like wealth, it's distributed to different groups, in different amounts." Keeping this analogy in mind, women as a group have historically been allotted especially measly portions of this pleasure stuff—you know, goodies like fattening food, orgasmic sex, money, and power. Though, now, finally, society is getting around to serving us women bigger platefuls—and we're not sure how to react, because we've been conditioned to expect so little.

Sharon, a copywriter, relates. She admits, "I remember how back in junior high school I felt embarrassed about my high grades. I started to feel this way later in my career about my high salary. I never used to allow myself to fully celebrate my accomplishments—because I didn't want those around me to feel bad. Now I figure I put up with a lot at the office. I deserve the satisfaction of feeling good about what I accomplish. In the last month, I've been talking more freely about my job, and it feels good. I figure if someone resents me for my success, this is not someone I want in my life."

It's strange how we make ourselves feel bad about feeling too good. I write about this in my novel, *50% Off*. In fact, here's that related quote now:

Some shameless self-promotion for my novel—that I refuse to feel guilty about indulging in.

In my novel Sasha Schwartz says, "I feel so happy, I can't stand it." Then Sasha wonders: "Why do we have expressions like that about happiness? Stuff like 'It's too much' or 'I could die.' It's like our language suggests we shouldn't let ourselves be happy too long. And then we also have expressions like: 'Everything in moderation' and 'Less is more' that idealize limiting happiness, as well as 'No pain, no gain!' to suggest there should be some punishment linked to happiness."

Missy, a successful real estate broker, agrees with my fictional heroine. "I was taught you have to struggle to get the good stuff," says Missy, "that the more miserable you are, the more pride you can take in your gains. Now I'm trying *not* to make myself feel bad about making money so easily, about taking shortcuts to my happiness."

Listen to Your Heart, Listen to Your Gut, Listen to NPR—But Stop Listening to Your Mother and/or That Obnoxious Colleague Down the Hall

*I*n your daily work life, you must resist the daily pushy and inappropriate requests of those around you—and stop feeling guilty about not doing everything everybody wants you to do. You must practice saying that tongue twister:

No.

You can't do everything or be everything to everybody. And you can't feel guilty about this fact either.

This guilt-free attitude also applies to the Big Picture: staying true to the career you want to pursue. Meaning, you must stay true to Principle #1 of the Master Plan, which says:

If you're gonna whip a career—whip your own career. Don't whip somebody else's.

Don't feel guilty about pursuing a different career path than Ma and Pa had scripted out for you since birth. Work is hard work—even if it's a career you love. And that goes quadruple for a career you hate. So remember, if you're going to spend your time and energy whipping a career, be sure it's over a career that turns *you* on when you whip it—and not your parental units.

Remember: You are the master of your career destiny—a master who refuses to limit yourself with restraining thoughts like: *What will others think? What will family-esque others think? What if I surpass my parents monetarily? Or let them down?*

Go for it. Seeking to achieve your own highest good is one of your God-given instincts—and I mean literally "God-given" and literally an "instinct."

You know how a flower instinctively goes toward the light to help it grow? A flower doesn't spend time worrying if people will mistake it for a weed or if it's taking too much sun. It wisely and simply follows its primal flower gut instincts to attain its highest level of flowerosity. You must do the same.

And so must I.

After all, being who you want to be, and doing what you want to do, is self-respect.

Or to quote Ayn Rand: "The achievement of his own happiness is man's highest moral purpose."

Meaning: Eating Ben and Jerry's New York Super Fudge after a hard day at the office is the moral thing to do.

Today's Fantasy Role-Playing Exercises
(and Tips for Cracking Whips)

Help! I Haven't a Thing to Aware

*T*oday make a date to talk with your parents and see what lessons you might have learned early on about expectations in your career life. This will help you develop insight into the role you play in preventing yourself from reaching and maintaining your objectives. Awareness is the first step to change. Sort of. Actually, awareness is the first step to depression. But eventually the change does come.

The Five-Sevenths Pleasure Principle

I am now writing a screenplay with my writing partner, Nancy—and having lots of fun in the process. Sometimes it even feels—dare I say—like too much fun. I've even joked with her that I feel guilty if I'm having too much fun while working because we're not getting enough work done. Or I feel guilty if I'm working too hard and we're not having enough fun. The lesson to be learned: *One must always find a way to feel guilty.* No, wait, that's not it. The lesson to be learned: It's okay to have fun at your job. In fact, if five days out of seven are spent working (if you're lucky—and not six days out of seven, if you live in Manhattan) at least five-sevenths of your life is spent on the job. You want to enjoy those five-sevenths as much as you can. Today take a fun break at your office—and don't feel guilty about it. Stretch your lunch out an extra 30 minutes, and treat yourself to dessert.

No-No's

Today, keep in mind Principle #9 of the Master Plan: You give someone enough rope, he'll tie you up with it. Go through the day listening especially closely to what people ask you to do at your job, and be ready to say *no* to someone who asks you to do something inappropriate. You know how to say *no*, don't you. You just put your lips together and . . . let it roll.

A Painful Question Now
That Will Lead to Pleasure Later

How does your long-term goal change when you remove guilt from mental programming? For instance, if you stopped caring what your mom or dad might say?

master mantras to help you whip

Guilt

into submission

Next time you feel like you've been guilting your own lily, remember:

1. I am not a SLAVE who gives people rope to tie me up with. I am a MASTER who controls what I do without getting tied up in guilt.

2. I am not a SLAVE who is restrained with childhood guilt. I am a MASTER who is on the train—riding first class—to success. Yihaa.

3. I am not a SLAVE who is held back by limited parental expectations. I am a MASTER who doesn't listen to the limiting views of how I was raised—and asks for raises.

4. I am not a SLAVE who keeps down with the Joneses. I am a MASTER who keeps up with my own long-term fantasy goal.

5. I am not a SLAVE who doesn't know how to say *no*. I am a MASTER who knows saying *no* can lead to more yeses.

Whip

Your Crazy Day

Into Submission

or

....

If the Coyote Had Stopped to Catch His Breath,
He Might Have Caught the Roadrunner

....

The other day I was doing my bills while watching a PBS special about transsexuals, and one thought—and one thought only—went racing through my mind:
Where do these people find the time to go for such an operation?

I can barely even find the time to do my bills let alone get new sexual organs. It seems I always have a list of 20 things to do, with time to do only 10, and I wind up doing 30.

Instead of Having Quality of Life
We Now Have *Quantity* of Life

So, how are we supposed to prioritize?
Especially when we are all in such constant motion, moving, spinning, filing, dialing, e-mailing, faxing, Starbucksing. With all this frenetic activity, we can miss out on the opportunity to clearly view our mistakes, define our priorities, and strategize a workable plan. Sometimes I feel I am keeping so outrageously busy that a green elf could be standing in the middle of my office waving a million bucks and the promise to free me from my work for the rest of my life—and I might not even notice.

So, what's a girl to do?

Take the Fat Out of Your Fate

I believe you face the same problems slimming down your weight, as slimming down your work schedule. This includes bad subconscious/conscious/unconscious habits, immediate gratification winning hands down in the popularity contest over long-term goal reaching.

Put Your Overstuffed Schedule—
and Psyche—on a Diet

You have a certain amount of energy to put into each day. Think of this energy as a "calorie allotment" and then think about how you want to use your calories in the following categories:

1. Actions—low-priority activities, high-priority activities, complaining, gossiping, meetings, phone calls, billings, filing, networking, etc.

2. Thoughts—guilt, worry, doubt, fear, regret, etc.
3. Distractions—sex, food, alcohol, drugs, money, over-working, etc.

If I'm not careful, I can find myself wasting a lot of my time calories in Categories #2 and #3, and not having enough time calories left over for the most important category: Category #1. And speaking of . . . I'm also hyper aware of how I use my time calories in this arena.

Selectivity Breeds Content

1. I'm aware that I work best during cusp times: first thing in the morning and late at night. You, too, should become aware of what your best hours are and create a sympathetic schedule. Are you an early-bird-catches-the-worm person or a night owl?

2. I'm aware of what the busiest hours of the day are for my career: writer. Around 10 o'clock I know editors start coming into the office. I know I can get my most writing done before 10. You too must become aware of what your busiest hours are in your career, and mold your schedule accordingly. Do your clients all seem to call after lunch? If so, make yourself available during this time zone.

3. I try to become aware—before I do anything—of which activities will lead me best to my long-term goal. Then I make sure *every day* I do at least one major thing to move myself toward my goal. You too must do the same. Don't let yourself get swept up in the minutiae. Maximize your time with your major priorities.

Become Proactive—and Pro-inactive

*J*ay, an entertainment lawyer at Paul Weiss, has a wildly busy schedule. Sometimes he gets so overwhelmed he has a hard time prioritizing. Whenever his brain gets so clogged up with activity he cannot think, he gets his feet moving. "I've found taking a ten-minute walk around the block can save me hours spinning my wheels at the office," says Jay. He understands an important principle about calorie expenditure. You can earn back more calories to use in your day—energy to spare—if you take time to relax.

Pam also knows yet another secret to getting extra freebie calories to spend:

Become a scan artist.

Pam, a film producer, recognizes she doesn't have time to read every script and every film industry publication that comes across her desk. So Pam has developed the art of scanning—reading the first chunk and the last chunk of each piece, recognizing that this is where the most important nutritional ingredients of knowledge can be found. She also trains her employees to know how to find good film scripts, and gives them a pile or two to read. Pam recognizes another important time-saver tip:

It's not just what you know, but how you get others to do stuff with what you know.

Another way to save calories in your day is to delegate, delegate, delegate. Decide which activities you can entrust to someone else in your office, and share and share alike.

All Talk Leads to No Action

Although it's good to have business associates to consult with during the day, you must watch out for time-wasting colleagues who gab and gab and gab . . . and distract you from your work at hand—and from remembering an important philosophical work concept: *You must work when you're working.*

Today's Fantasy Role-Playing Exercises
(and Tips for Cracking Whips)

Deadlines, Injured-Lines, and End-of-the-Lines

Today, look at your work goals for the next three months. Create a workable schedule to meet your goals by setting a three-tiered-deadline system based on the following system: injured-line, deadline, end-of-the-line. An injured-line is your first stab at finishing a project, a deadline is when you *feel* it's done, and end-of-the-line is the killer truth of when it's due. Mark them in your calendar. By writing it down you are activating your subconscious mind, and reinforcing your determination.

Zen Rock and Bowl

There's a famous Zen puzzle that serves as a metaphor for demonstrating how to prioritize better: Pretend you have to fill a bowl with large rocks, pebbles, sand, and water. If you put the small things in first, it would overflow. The only way to fill the bowl without it overflowing is to start with the largest rocks, then add the pebbles around the side of the bowl, then add the sand in between the pebbles, then add the water. The same thing goes with filling your business day. The big important things must come first. Take your "to do" list for this week and separate out the rocks from the pebbles.

Instead of "Sit Ups," Do "Sit Downs"

*S*it down for 15 minutes and burn off some fat in your schedule and psyche by answering the following: What are your most productive hours? What are your business's busiest periods where you should make yourself most available? What people, thoughts, and distractions are wasting calories in your day-to-day schedule? Now, knowing all of the above, how can you work more efficiently?

It's Better to Have a Hen Tomorrow Than an Egg Now

*T*oday look at your schedule and determine—honestly— which activities will lead you to your long-term goal most expediently. Draw a little cartoon of a hen next to these most important activities—then draw an egg next to the lesser ones.

Elevator Music to Your Ears

*T*oday decide to use any waiting time for elevators—or movies, restaurants, restrooms—even call waiting—to your most positive advantage. Don't use this time full of anxiety about having to wait. Instead use it to solve a work problem or repeat a positive Master Mantra. Perhaps even one of the following:

master mantras to help you whip

Your Crazy Day

into submission

Next time you feel your schedule getting wildly out of control, remember:

1. I am not a SLAVE who is controlled by time. I am a MASTER who controls time so it serves me well.

2. I am not a SLAVE who gets tied up in busywork. I am a MASTER who lassos work so my day works for me.

3. I am not a SLAVE who is running constantly in circles. I am a MASTER who runs circles around others at my office.

4. I am not a SLAVE who loses track of time. I am a MASTER who keeps track of my deadlines.

5. I am not a SLAVE who is dominated by lesser priorities. I am a MASTER who is in control of my priorities and knows which are dominant.

Whip *Jealousy* *Into Submission*

or

....

You Must Avoid "What-You-See" Sickness

....

Pssssst. I have something to confess. Whenever I read articles about other writers, I always check out their ages, and if they're much younger than me and already a *New York Times* bestseller—and thinner—well, I must admit, I feel myself getting a bit green around my edges.

Actually, I believe we can find out our true values and priorities not by engaging in warm fuzzy talks with friends, but by watching what gets us riled up with jealousy. For instance, I can hear that someone was named head of the neurosurgery department at a hospital, and feel nothing. Nada. However, if I hear about someone getting to direct his first feature film, well, admittedly I can feel a bit of that green aura start to surround me. This cause-and-effect system is good news for anyone who's not sure what he wants to do with his life. This means that whenever the jealousy alarms are sounded, you can almost know for sure you're in the presence of something you really want.

Okay. So then what, you may ask. What next?

Actually there are—in total:

Three Kinds of Jealousy / Three Kinds of Responses

1. Low-grade jealousy—you want what the other person has, but feel low self-esteem about getting it. For instance, a photographer friend is getting all the coolest assignments in fashion magazines, but you're a lawyer and don't feel you have it in you to be a photographer.
2. High-grade jealousy—you not only want what the other person has, you really don't want him to have it either. For instance, you are a photographer and feel a competitor is less talented yet getting more work.
3. Positive jealousy—you're fine with the other person having what he has because it serves as proof that what you want can be gotten, and thereby you allow your jealousy to inspire the attainment of your desire. You're a photographer who is jealous of a competitor's workload so you work at improving your portfolio so you can improve the odds of getting better assignments.

Hopefully you are of the third ilk, and not of the other two icks (that's short for icky).

You—as a master of your destiny—must learn to master jealousy. I have. Yup. Jealousy R NOT Us. There. Does that make you jealous of me and thereby make you want to learn to master jealousy faster? If not . . . here's:

$\mathscr{A}$ good antidote to poison envy.

It helps to remember that no matter what another has, there are always tradeoffs. Like in the movie *The Turning Point,* the woman who pursued dancing was jealous of the woman who pursued a family life—and vice versa. In the end they both realized that each path had its share of difficulties, making each of them a little less jealous of the other—and that the path they each chose was right for each of them. Actually all Hollywood "switch" movies make this point: *Trading Places, Tootsie, Big, The Crying Game* (well, maybe that one's a stretch).

It's a Cat-Eat-Cat World

$\mathscr{W}$e women can sometimes be worse at handling jealousy than men for a few reasons:

1. Women are confused by our choices of destinies—mommy, or career woman, or single and living a wild sexual adventure, or married and monotonous—uh, I meant monogamous. Anyway . . . It's easy to feel as if we've picked the wrong path.
2. Women are less trained in the art of healthy competition than men because until recently we weren't offered the same opportunities in sports growing up. We do have one advantage: We master shopping—which can be a sport in itself—especially in the big discount houses like Loehmanns, where it's every woman for herself. Take no prisoners.
3. Women in business have a scarcity mentality—we feel there are fewer good jobs to go around for us, so we're even more sensitized to someone else having a desirable job that we feel (often paranoiacally) is limited in its distribution . . . like I often feel is true about those

size six Donna Karan suits at Loehmanns—which I'm always missing out on.

Anyway, all of the above can lead a woman into the ol' . . .

"I Think Therefore I Am . . . a Loser" Syndrome

*Y*ou must not beat yourself up with negative thoughts of jealousy, you must beat them instead. Whenever you feel jealous, yearning for someone else's six-figure income, or humongous corner office with the great view of the apartment building across the street where it seems young, hot newlyweds are cohabitating—hourly—and so then you also become jealous of the young cohabitating newlyweds—just remember: *We live in a world of abundance.* There are enough good jobs to go around for everyone—and enough discounted size six Donna Karan suits. You just have to keep wielding your whip at destiny until destiny submits and gives you what you want. You must always remember that having a MASTER MENTALITY is a more powerful determining factor in getting the job of your dreams (or the Donna Karan suit of your fantasies) than any statistics you hear about.

The trick is to be *persistent,* and recognize that the person you are jealous of—who has what you want—probably had to go through a lot of pain and struggle to get it—even if it doesn't seem that way on the surface. Yes, you may feel as if you are being singled out by the fates to suffer. But everyone on this planet Earth experiences major disappointments and pain—even that person with the senior VP title, the corner office, and the discounted size six Donna Karan suit.

The Grass is Greener on the Other Side—Until You Get There and See That It's Astroturf

*A*nother thing a master keeps DOMINANT in her mind: *Symbols are not reality.* Someone might have amassed material success, but this doesn't mean he's happy. So don't judge a book by its cover. You must read at least 53 pages of *The Book of Who Someone Is* to know where he is at. Things aren't always as they seem.

As we all know, there are many successful people—John Belushi and Marilyn Monroe, for example—who seemed as if they had it made, but were coming undone at the seams. And look at O.J. Before the murders, people thought he was a guy who had it all. One Bronco ride later, they had to think again. And then there was the time I saw Cindy Crawford up close at my gym. Let me tell you—you know how people say models are absolutely nothing without good makeup, lighting, and air-brushing? Well, I saw Cindy naked and without makeup and the poor girl is—well—she is incredible-looking. I didn't eat for three weeks.

But then again, I have things going for me that Cindy doesn't have.

I'm sure.

I bet.

Um . . .

For instance, I probably have a better self-deprecatory sense of humor than Cindy has.

You know what? When it comes right down to it, for as much of a bummer as it may be, you can't have everything in this world. You just have to make sure you have the right some-things.

Each of Us Has Her Own Gifts— and They're Not One-Size-Fits-All

*N*o one of us is on the same path. We each have different talents, goals, needs, dress sizes, shoe sizes, food preferences, food allergies, pet peeves, pet names, etc. Feeling competitive with what someone else has can sidetrack you from what you— as a unique individual—with your own personalized monogrammed long-term goals—may want.

For instance, Kelly and Marcy (not their real names) are two sisters (actually they're brothers) who were always competitive with each other (that part is true). They both went into law—although Marcy was always the more creative one. Marcy just wanted to do what her sister did—and hopefully do it better. Finally Marcy realized she didn't want what her sister had, but wanted a career as an illustrator. She quit the law firm and now does illustration for a living—and is much happier making less money but pursuing her unique career path—and she attained this satisfaction only once she let go of all that competitive jealousy.

You Must Beat Yourself at Your Own Game— Without Beating Yourself Up

*D*on't compete with others. Compete with yourself. Actually there's a *Cosmo* print ad that has a great slogan we should all memorize:

Anything I can do I can do better.

You must de-focus on the competition and refocus on your fabulous skills and your long-term goals. So, instead of being jealous of what your boss does at the office, start thinking of yourself as the understudy for your boss, and start improving the skills you'll need to someday do his job.

Emerson said, "What lies behind us and what lies in front of us pales in comparison to what lies in us." You have inside you tremendous potential and power. *If you want to get more pull at your office you've got to push yourself.* Be a pushy broad. Push yourself to improve your job skills about 3 percent each day. Push yourself to stay focused on what you're doing instead of how others are doing. Push yourself to stay positive. With conscious awareness, you can make your emotions serve you—and serve you well, like the good stuff, like the Ben and Jerry's New York Fudge ice cream of thoughts.

Today's Fantasy Role-Playing Exercises (and Tips for Cracking Whips)

Jealousy Barometer Exercise

Today when you read your daily newspaper or magazine, be aware of what makes you jealous. Write it down. Then decide to attain it.

Bound (and Gagged) for Success

Don't brag. It doesn't get you anywhere except a place of resentment from others who will become jealous of you. So be humble and mumble about your successes—particularly to those you feel are particularly susceptible to breaking out from poison envy.

Get an Envy League Education

A person who has what you want is a person you can learn from. So today decide to read a biography of a famous person who has managed to do something you always wanted to do. Check out the stories of Bill Gates and Coco Chanel, to name two interesting tales of triumph over troubles.

Convert Your Neuroses Into Found Money

A re you constantly thinking about all the treasures those around you have that you have *not?* If so, remember: Jealousy will not bring them any closer to you. If you want to increase your career luck, increase your long-term goal focus. Next time you find yourself getting all caught up with jealous thoughts, get yourself thinking about something you want. For instance: What am I going to do with all my millions of dollars once I get it? Erasmus said: A nail is driven out by another nail; habit is overcome by habit. I say: You can nail that raise by developing the habit of positive thinking.

master mantras to help you whip

Jealousy

into submission

Next time you feel a little green jealousy creep into your system, flush it out by remembering:

1. I am not a SLAVE who wants what others have. I am a MASTER who knows what I want and goes for it.

2. I am not a SLAVE who sees the grass as greener on the other side. I am a MASTER who waters my positive thoughts about my career so they bloom into reality.

3. I am not a SLAVE who wishes I were Cindy Crawford. I am a MASTER who wishes I were Cindy Crawford. Wait. That's not what I meant. I am a MASTER who is happy with being who I am because I have my own unique talents that Cindy is lacking, poor girl.

4. I am not a SLAVE who thinks there's not enough good stuff to go around. I am a MASTER who makes the rounds until I get the good stuff.

5. I am not a SLAVE who tortures myself with comparisons to others. I am a MASTER who turns myself on with what I am doing.

Whip

Change

Into Submission

or

....

When You Grow, You Outgrow—or a Job
May Outgrow How It Starts to Grow

....

W hen I was having my apartment painted, it went through a period of time where it looked . . . well . . . horrifying. All the furniture was piled up earthquake style. Paint-splattered dropcloths were flung everywhere. The place was a wreck.

Luckily I knew where all this change was leading—to a more beautiful apartment.

Well, change in your career suffers from the same myopic difficulties. Sometimes you can only see how bad things look, when they're really on their way to looking better.

Really.

Just ask Hillary.

Who's Hillary?

Well, I can tell you who's she's *not* anymore. She *used* to be a senior vice president in charge of marketing at a small cosmetics company, loving her job. Then one day she was told that her entire company was moving to Paris. After much debate—with her boss, her boyfriend, and her inner demons—she turned down the move—and her company told her she had to find another job.

"At first I panicked," said Hillary, "I worried where/how/when my next job would come. Then I disciplined my mind to focus instead on my talents, what skills I uniquely have, why I'd be highly hireable. I told myself this was an opportunity to get an even better, higher-paying, more satisfying job. I got myself totally psyched. Plus, I also focused on how I'd gotten my present job unexpectedly. It could happen again."

It did.

Sure enough, six months later Hillary bumped into someone at a business function who told her about a phenomenal job opportunity with a perfume company. Hillary interviewed, got the job, and finds it far more satisfying (both creatively and monetarily) than her previous position.

Hillary understood what every dominatrix of her destiny understands: You must not worry over things that must change. Worry is a worthless emotion. Let it go. Put it in a drawer. Or better yet, throw it out. You must accept the following truth right now:

The only constant in life is change.

Your career (or even goals) can change at any time. [Like this typeface.] Or this language . . . *voilà! si! bfrgrkp mjpo?* into a language you cannot understand. Which I suppose is our worst fear: not understanding something—for example, why must something change?

Believe me, I understand how difficult career change can be. I've changed my career many times. I've been an actress, an ad writer, a book writer, a screenwriter—even a ventriloquist. When I was 12, I performed ventriloquism at children's parties. Sometimes when the writing life gets rough, I calm my weary nerves with the cheery reminder that I always have my ventriloquism career to fall back upon.

My point: I personally know how hard it is to deal with a career's vicissitudes. It's even harder to know how to spell vicissitudes. (I looked it up.) I was recently talking about career vicissitudes with Nina, a teacher of the Alexander Technique—which is the quintessential study of body movement, awareness, and posture. She showed me a wonderful metaphor for dealing with it: "broom balancing." Nina explained, "If you want to balance a broom handle on the palm of your hand, you must be aware of how the broom is moving and be ready to move and adapt with the movements of the broom—*move with how it moves.*"

I have often experienced the career version of this technique. For instance, I had a screenplay idea I told to a TV producer friend, who thought it would make a great TV show. So I restructured the idea for television, then sold it to Nickelodeon. Unfortunately, it never made it to series. But I—being the dominatrix of my destiny—took *this* script and reworked it as a children's book, drawing my own illustrations—enabling me to use a talent I never would have been able to show with a TV or movie script. And now my agent recently got some interest in this book from a publishing house!

You Must See a Change as a Chance

*C*hange is really an opportunity to evolve to a better place.

The trick is to remain clear about your true goals, but flexible in how to achieve them. My true goal: Create work I'm proud of. My flexibility: It can be in the form of film, TV, or books.

The key thing to always keep in mind is:

Your career life is not your master, it is your slave.

It's up to you to tell your career life what to do. When unexpected circumstances arise, it's up to you to transform any changes into changes for the best. Don't just take what comes to you. Go out there and see the marketplace for what it is. Learn what's out there. You must keep an open mind *and* remember to keep in mind: *You're not in this world to serve a career goal you've made for yourself; it's your job that's simply one mechanism for fulfilling your true happiness.*

Are You in Hot Water?

*M*argaret Atwood once wrote about how a person can boil to death in a bathtub if the water temperature is turned up hotter and hotter in slow enough increments. You might not notice the water getting to boiling point, and then—croak. Sometimes your career can—without your realizing it—enter into this boiling zone, too.

You're working hard, dealing with the day-to-day job, watching colleagues move up and move out, clinking glasses at going-away parties, congratulating your office mate on her move to Florida. Then suddenly you look around and you see you have a different boss, different clients, different colleagues, different company morale—a whole different company. And you realize: You are unhappy with all these differences. And for a good reason. After all, who you work *for* and work *with* can be far more important than what you *do*. If who you work for and work with sucks, then your job sucks.

Sure, for a while you might want to try to stick things out with these new sucky people, thinking you can help these people to change into unsucky people—but this, my dear reader, is thinking that is representative of the rarest phenomenon in all nature: *getting others to change.* (Mistress Karen has foolishly attempted this in her love life with men as well, and has concluded the following universal truth: The only thing you can ever expect to change in a man is—*maybe*—his wardrobe.)

But while trying to get others to change is like pounding your head against a wall—only not nearly as much fun—luckily you do have the power to do something incredibly earth-shattering, that is at the same time easily do-able: *Change your own circumstance.*

Here are two famous quotes to use as inspiration for your next steps:

1. You can't steal second if you keep a foot on first.
2. Jump and the net will appear.

I love both of the above, and firmly believe that if what you're doing is not something you like, then leave. Life is too short to be doing things you do not like. We dominatrixes recognize this and know not to be afraid to pursue the required change—because we know that our gut instincts will prevail, that we are in control of our destinies.

To Be Able to Move Sideways Rather Than Forward Is a Much Braver Path

You know how people are always raving about the divinity of stick-to-itiveness? I say: Fuck it. It's a much bolder to unstick yourself from a job or any situation that is not working anymore.

The Buddhists stress that it's good to let go and not have too many attachments.

For as much as it's good to know what you want and who

you want to be, paradoxically it's also good to be open to letting go of any attachments to your career or who you think you are. Here are two words to explain why:

Beta VCRs.

And here are another two words:

Bell bottoms.

Obviously the above fashion statement could only have been created during a time people were doing massive psychedelics. I mean: What were these fashion designers thinking? HOWEVER . . . What if we had been unwilling as a society to accept the "letting go" of bell bottoms?

Perhaps you are in a bell bottom job now. You know, one of those seemingly hot trendy consulting or Internet-related jobs that you kind of fell into after graduation because everyone you know was moving to San Francisco and it all sounded so cool but then you realized that you were sick of talking about "synergy" and "speed to market" and started looking lovingly at law school applications. If so, it's time to take off those "career bell bottoms" (hey, it may be a great job for some people, but only some people look great in weirdly shaped pants, you know?), remind yourself of what you really want to be doing with your 10-hour workday (and be thinking about for the other 14 hours), and make a career transformation. In other words, maybe it's time to try a new career on for size.

A Master Recognizes That She Can Wear Many Hats in This Lifetime—and Sometimes on the Weekend a Matching G-string

Though that last bit is another story. Anyway . . . A master is always ready and open and listening for all kinds of new experiences—job-wise as well as otherwise.

However, there is one thing to keep in mind if you are going

to change jobs. You will have to undergo a learning curve, so
don't take the bumps of learning new stuff too hard. You can't
rip the skin off a snake. The snake must moult. You must accept
that you're moulting as fast you can.

Bob Dylan said it well when he said: "He who's not busy being born is busy dying."

In other words, it's important to view change as an opportunity to grow in new ways (and not just focus on all the growing
pains).

Which reminds me of a story:

Leader of the Pack

*My dad and I were talking about what makes for a success-
ful business person, and he told me about this poster he got
at one of his stockbroker conventions that said: "Winning is
an attitude." He was coming to visit me in NY that weekend,
and he said he would bring me the poster. Unfortunately, he
spoke too soon. When he went to pack the poster into his
suitcase, it didn't fit. The poster was too large, the suitcase
too stuffed. He was about to give up. But then he saw those
words staring up at him: "Winning is an attitude." So he
tried again with a bit more ferocity.*

It fit.

I got the poster.

And I want YOU to be the poster child for that poster.

Winning IS an attitude, and an important attitude to keep in
mind when change strikes.

Or to quote the Rolling Stones: "You can't always get what
you want . . . but you get what you need."

Today's Fantasy Role-Playing Exercises
(and Tips for Cracking Whips)

Be a Closet Case

*T*oday throw out all the things in your closet you don't wear. It will serve as an inspiring metaphor for why it's important to "let go." You will visually see how you are opening up space for new things to come in—as well as visually see how you have changed when it comes to what you choose to wear—hopefully not because you've changed too much in the cellulite department. Speaking of which. Repeat this existential experience with the stuff in your refrigerator you don't eat. (I mean, meatloaf is not supposed to be purple.)

Is It Time to Get a Raise or Rise a Rung?

*M*ark, now a CEO, told me one of his career tips was to "always be looking for the next promotion." Today think about what you want to change at your present job and then keep in mind: Ask and ye shall receive.

A Painful Question Now
That Will Lead to Much Pleasure Later

I started my career at JWT as a junior copywriter. I realized a way to grow up more quickly in my career was to leave agencies. I would immediately lose my "junior" aura and get more power. So I left and went to McCann Erickson across the street and quickly got put on more senior accounts. Have you been in the same place too long? What would happen if you spread your wings and winged it to another company?

master mantras 5 *to help you whip*

Change

into submission

Next time you don't want to let go, stop and remember:

1. I am not a SLAVE who wears blinders to the office. I am a MASTER who sees my career life for what it is.

2. I am not a SLAVE who sees changes as stumbling blocks in my life path. I am a MASTER who sees changes as stepping stones to help me climb another rung higher up the career ladder—and/or the knowledge ladder.

3. I am not a SLAVE who refuses to let go. I am a MASTER who has get up and go.

4. I am not a SLAVE who thinks change sucks. I am a MASTER who sucks the most out of change.

5. I am not a SLAVE who gets turned on by limited thinking about who I can be. I am a MASTER who gets excited by dressing up in new career hats—and wielding that career whip.

Whip Intuition

Into Submission

or

....

What You Don't See Is What You Get

....

Ironically, the best advertising campaign I ever wrote was
one that I had to do under pressure, overnight. Because I
was lacking in time, I couldn't waste frivolous hours over-
thinking, second-guessing my every word. I had to think on
my feet, feel with my gut, trust my intuition.

And that was the first ad I won a Clio for. And right now I'd
like to take the time to thank intuition for making it all possible.
Thank you. Cocktails will be served in the other room.

Intuition Rules

As a master of your destiny you must learn to listen to your
feelings, and recognize that they are incognito business

confidantes that will always supply ample important information like: Don't trust that goofball client. Call that employee now and make sure he understands how to run that computer. Your zipper is down. *Definitely absolutely, totally* don't trust that goofball client.

Of course it's scary to rely on intuition, because it doesn't feel real. It's not anything tangible that you can point to, like an umbrella or a carburetor. It's invisible—but then again, so is odorless gas, yet it has the power to change your life (kill you). And look at television. It's merely a box with wires. Yet when invisible energy passes through it, it, too, has the power to change your life (kill your taste level).

So what's it to you to believe in yet one more invisible thing like intuition?

I know, I know—*I know.* At first intuition sounds weird, freaky, psychedelic, man—but it explains a lot of the weird/ freaky/psychedelic, man things that happen. For instance, intuition is that all-knowing energy that dogs tap into when they sense an earthquake coming—and what a mom taps into when even from a distance she can sense her baby is in danger—and what you tap into when you think about your boss and what a dink he is and a moment later he calls you on the phone and says something dinky.

It's also what you rely on when you're in a life-threatening situation. You use it to do what you gotta do instinctively to survive. It's these very same survival instincts that you should be relying on daily to help you do what you gotta do to survive an unfortuitous business meeting or an overanalyzed report. Let go and feel your response. Use your gut.

Or in some cases, even your *back.*

Turning Pain Into Pleasure

George Soros, a billionaire investor, wrote in his book *Soros on Soros*, "I rely a great deal on animal instincts. When I was actively running the Fund, I suffered from backaches. I used the onset of acute pain as a signal that there was something wrong in my portfolio."

A lot of the world's most successful people trust their bodies as much as their brains.

Robin, a garment buyer (or "garmento," as the slang goes) says, "I used to overthink problems at the office—like wondering if I was imagining that a colleague was trying to take over part of my work territory. I'd analyze the details of their behavior that I'd collected, then spend hours on end thinking about it. Now I realize that my body is smarter than my brain. If I get a stomachache around certain people, I listen to it. Or if someone just makes me feel anxious to be around them, I pay attention. I recognize that the same way I trust my instincts to know what shoes go with what dress go with what handbag—I don't question it, overthink it, I just know—well, I know what I know when it comes to people and business, too."

Think Less, Feel More

It's funny how we use intuition all the time shopping and dating, trusting our instincts on what clothes to buy and what sexual come-on lines from suitors to buy into. But we are afraid to use these same instincts in business. We think we have to listen to our rational brains and back up everything with facts—that may or may not be true as time passes, anyway.

Some Good Business Advice
That Seems Like Vice but Isn't

1. Be thoughtless.
2. Be out of your mind.

What I Mean by This

*Y*ou must relearn not to live too much in your mind, rely on your intellect too much for guidance.

You know how it's a lost cause if you struggle too hard to remember someone's name? That's because you're putting too much strain on your brain. Sometimes you just have to relax and let things come to you. That's what I do in my business, whenever I'm having a creative block with writing. And that's what you should do with your business. Just sit back, close your eyes (note: Don't try this if your business requires operating heavy machinery) and let the answer slowly, calmly, intuitively—brainlessly—come to you.

Intuition: The Perfect Present

*I*ntuition is not to be confused with psychic ability. It's not about seeing into the future, *it's about seeing into the present.* And let me tell you, this present-tense vision at first glance might seem easy, but it is far from it.

When you are able to master being fully in the present you can fully listen to your back and belly and heart and pick up tons of energy data—emotionally, psychologically, spiritually—that will help you make the right decisions. Intuition shows up in many familiar forms that you might not originally recognize, like the aforementioned backaches and stomachaches, as well as depression, headaches, fatigue, nightmares, anxiety, and digestive problems. So if any of these are troubling any of you LISTEN UP.

Basically intuition is your God-given animal instincts. We humans have them because we are animals—just like an armadillo—only we don't know how to use them nearly as effectively as an armadillo. When an armadillo senses danger, it instinctively runs or attacks (it doesn't sit there and get an ulcer). When an armadillo is hungry, it instinctively uses its primal senses to track down its prey, stalk it, then go in for the kill (it doesn't consult a bunch of friends for their opinions or convene a focus group). An armadillo has one up on you because it wisely knows how to recognize its emotions as a warning or as a guide or as information to be utilized.

A Day in the Life of Intuition

*L*aura Day, author of *Practical Intuition*, makes her living from cashing in on her intuition. She is hired by doctors, lawyers, CEOs, politicians, investors, and actors to help them master their intuition so they can better figure out how to handle their careers. She also uses it to forecast the stock market, diagnose illnesses, develop courtroom strategies—even bet on horses. Plus, it seems writing a book all about intuition was a bit of good intuition—it landed her on the *New York Times* bestseller list.

Laura Day believes that we all, through daily practice, can learn to fully develop our intuition and cash in on it at the office by better understanding those mysterious unfathomable creatures called clients, colleagues, and bosses. We just have to learn to respect this God-given instinct more, see it as being a rational business tool rather than a woo-woo pseudoscience.

Never Kid a Kid

*W*e first learn to push down our intuition in childhood when we are told that something we think we see—like Mom crying in the kitchen, Dad drinking his fourth vodka tonic, brother wearing Mommy's housedress in the bathroom—is not true. As adults, we have to learn to reown our belief in what we think is true. We're told to blatantly ignore what's right in front of us, and are even punished sometimes when we point it out. So we learn from an early age to capitulate to the "wink-wink," it's-not-really-there practice of our highers up. It starts with our parents, then manifests itself in business situations.

We can often find ourselves caring too much what others think, and we stop valuing what *we* see and feel. Instead, we're paying too much attention to the opinions of the guy with the corner office or the woman with our paycheck. We learn it's better to keep quiet if we see something wrong with an idea or a way of approaching a problem. If our bosses don't speak up or even seem to be supporting a direction we see as flawed, instead of saying, "Are you crazy?" we freeze up and talk ourselves out of voicing our bullshit-meter opinion.

Bringing Intuition to Fruition

*T*here is one cure for a nonfunctioning intuition: Build up your self-esteem. When it comes right down to it, it's low self-esteem that ultimately keeps you from listening to yourself, and trusting your instincts. It's when you don't have enough faith in yourself and your feelings, that you find yourself insecurely asking everyone else's opinions—a practice that will not get you respect or leadership opportunities in the business world—just a big phone bill.

Once you start building up your confidence, you'll find that you'll be simultaneously building up your intuition skills. When you do, you'll find you are more and more in the *right* place, at the *right* time, wearing the *right* outfit, with all the *right* business associates fawning at your feet (both the *right* of your feet, and the left).

Today's Fantasy Role-Playing Exercises
(and Tips for Cracking Whips)

A Dream Career

Start a dream diary and write down your nightly homemade mental movies. Your subconscious might be trying to send you some messages about your career that you should pay attention to.

Finding Things That Push Your Belly Button

Make a list of the top five people you come into contact with most in business. Now quickly write down—stream of consciousness style—all your thoughts and feelings on these people. Do you trust them? Think they know what they're talking about? Are they on top of their game?

So, Are You "In Tu It"—or Not?

You must be into trying to be more in tu it. Practice using your intuition a little each day—or else, if your intuition doesn't feel like you're paying attention to it, eventually it will go away. Today listen to what your body tells you. Are there times you feel your gut tense up or a headache seize you? Susie, a writer friend, has a saying: "You must let yourself know what you know." So what do you know today?

master mantras to help you whip

Intuition

into submission

Next time you feel you want to punch down a hunch, re-member:

1. I am not a SLAVE who doesn't listen to what my belly may be telling me. I am a MASTER who thinks from my gut.

2. I am not a SLAVE who lets others' opinions control me. I am a MASTER who is in control of what I feel and think.

3. I am not a SLAVE who thinks but doesn't feel. I am a MASTER who thinks feeling is an important business tool.

4. I am not a SLAVE who doesn't trust my gut. I am a MASTER who has the guts to trust my gut.

5. I am not a SLAVE who doesn't trust my instincts. I am MASTER who instinctively reacts and acts.

Whip

Indecision

Into Submission

or

If You're Gonna Swing, Swing Hard

There were many times I was ready to give up writing my novel, when I was exhausted, or frustrated, or insecure, or miffed, or hungry for a cheeseburger and fries. Each time I was ready to give up, I'd tell myself: Right now some other writer is about to give up—but if *I* keep on going, I am *that* much closer to being the novelist who catches some editor's eye. Then I'd motivate myself the same way I do when running long distances: if I can just get to that next tree. Then I'd get to that "next tree" of my novel, and keeping running.

I was determined.

I had made the internal decision: I will be published.

Same goes with Marty, a music manager. He loved music and working with musicians. He started his career first as an assistant, then worked his way up at a big record label. But all along he secretly harbored the fantasy of managing talent some-day. He gobbled up every bit of information about the music business—and business in general—that he could at his job. After years in a splashy corporate job, he quit to start up Little Big Man. "The first few years were rocky," says Marty, "I thought at times that my business might even go under. But I was determined to gather some talented people into my fold—then the next thing I knew I had Sarah McLaughlin, then the Lilith festival, then the Verve—and my business just keeps growing and growing. I'm looking into getting biggger office space. I have the company of my dreams and I love it. I just totally love what I do for a living. I feel so lucky."

One-Track Mind

*M*arty's luck came from being decisive: He had made up his mind that nothing would stop him from reaching his career goal.

John Stuart Mill wrote: "One person with a belief is equal to a force of ninety-nine who have only interests." Just as there are no wishy-washy CEOs or wishy-washy astronauts or wishy-washy Joffrey Ballet dancers, there are no wishy-washy industry leaders in whatever your career fantasy may be.

A Checkered Future

*D*o you know the rules of the game of checkers? The first is that one must not make two moves at once. The second is that one may only move forward and not backward. And the third is that when one has reached the last row, one may move wherever one likes."—Martin Buber.

This quote reminds me of something that underappreciated Zen philosopher Bazooka Joe said: "Never compromise your dreams."

Bazooka Joe is right—and pretty deep for a bubble gum guy.

Sometimes indecision can display itself as compromise: We go back and forth telling ourselves that getting halfway to our career fantasy is enough. For instance, Marty could have told himself that since he had made it in the door at the hoity-toity music company, that counted as getting his fantasy career. But in reality that would have been indecision disguised as compromise.

What compromise is about is the fear that the world will not provide for you, because:

1. You fear the world is inadequate.
2. You fear you are inadequate.
3. You fear taking full mature (ugh) responsibility for your life.

For instance, right now you might feel kinda okay about your job. So you could start to tell yourself that it's no big deal not to ask for that promotion—or there's no major rush to start interviewing. After all, you are doing pretty well as a junior accountant, or marketing supervisor, or assistant to the big cheese. But you should keep in mind this brilliant thought somebody—I don't know who—said sometime, somewhere:

The greatest enemy of the great is the good.

Meaning: If you cowardly settle for accepting only the sevens life has to give you, then you won't live a ten life. Even if you gather a million seven-level jobs, because you'll still be creating a median of a seven life. Not a ten life.

Groucho Marx joked about marrying an unattractive mate because a beautiful one could leave you. His friend reminded him: "An ugly one could you leave you, too." Groucho agreed, but explained, "Yeah, but if they do, who cares."

Same with jobs . . .

By picking the safe and lesser job, you lessen your fear of losing it someday and being all distraught—however, you also 100 percent lessen your chance of getting your dream job in the first place.

So make up your mind what it is you want to do, then make up your mind to be brave about pursuing it.

Part of Luck Comes from Thinking About What You Want Soooo Much That It Has No Choice but to Materialize

*M*adonna—the material girl—used determination to help her career materialize. Madonna was so poor when she first moved to New York that she even ate food out of trashcans, plucking out half-finished Twinkies with her lace gloves. But she didn't let a little poverty stop her from getting one the most provocative, extravagantly indulgent, highest-paying careers on this planet. She began it all by pulling all-nighters, making her demo tape in the wee hours, when recording-studio sessions were cheapest, then pounding feistily on hundreds of doors trying to get someone (like a Marty type) to listen to it.

The Greater Your Decisiveness, the Greater Your Energy and Enthusiasm, and Thereby the Greater Your Luck

*E*very huge leap ahead in a career comes after a clear, committed decision to get to the other side of any hurdles in front of you—and you can only get over those hurdles with decisiveness.

"When I finally made up my mind that I wanted to produce films for a living, many people told me it would be impossibly difficult," says Lauren, now a senior VP in charge of producing many of MTV's most highly rated and most highly awarded programs. "I recognized that TV networks would be a good source for work—and in particular MTV, who I heard wanted to produce provocative, visually exciting product. So when I met someone at a party who worked there, I saw it as an act of fate, and invited them to a screening of my film from grad school, which was playing at the Museum of Modern Art. I was determined to get in the door at MTV." Ten years later, Lauren heads up MTV's documentary department, producing about 52 documentaries a year. "When I stop to think about it—when I have time to stop and think about it—I realize this is a dream job."

You Must Make Your Burning Desire Be the Light at the End of the Tunnel

$\mathcal{M}$e personally, I wrote 28 drafts of my novel—over a span of two years—until I felt it was ready to be sent to agents. Tina, a successful designer, interviewed at 27 different design companies before she got her present fantasy career, designing product packaging and logos. Colonel Sanders knocked on 1,009 doors before he sold his now-famous chicken recipe.

Me, Tina, and the Colonel all know: It's not easy. You've got to be determined. It's not enough to *mildly* want your fantasy career goal—you must *wildly* want it. Just like for a relationship to fully work you must be fully committed, for a career to fully work you must be fully committed.

Taking No Action Is a Choice

You must face an important truth: If you do nothing to move your career in the direction of your fantasies, you are still doing something. You are making the decision to stay in the same place. Each day I wasn't a novelist, for instance, I was more and more an advertising person. So indirectly, indecision still is a method to choose your career—but in the opposite direction than determination.

There are many tricks you can use to make sure you sustain your indecision. One of them is to keep asking people what they think you should do. Although I believe it's good to gather counsel from your loved ones, you must keep in mind, each time you do, you get a petri dish of others' projections along with it.

Consider Halle's situation. "My mother kept telling me how hard it is for a woman to become head resident at a hospital—especially a black woman," says Halle. "I knew this was her own insecurities talking. If I had listened to her, I wouldn't now be a head resident."

So, if you ask counsel from others on your career, make sure it's from somebody who believes in the pursuit of one's dreams, not somebody who will be talking from his own disappointments or fears or insecurities—or from a different generation that brings with it different perspectives on women—or other prejudicial views. (Which reminds me . . . You know what I often wonder: Why it is that single girls are always giving dating advice to *other single girls.* Isn't that like a guy who's loaded advising the guy sitting on the barstool next to him on the secrets of how to stop drinking?)

Today's Fantasy Role-Playing Exercises
(and Tips for Cracking Whips)

Master Recall

Today page through some magazines looking for words or pictures of people who are consistent with your fantasy goal. Tape them into your journal. Whenever you're feeling indecisive, turn to these pages of your journal for inspiration.

Don't Be Chicken—but Do Eat It

Today visit a Colonel Sanders (now known in the nineties as KFC) and ask the person behind the counter for a bucket of fried chicken legs—and a list of how many locations they have in your city. Then ask them how many locations they have around the world. Remember, Colonel Sanders knocked on 1,009 doors. If he had stopped at 1,008 there wouldn't be a Colonel Sanders where you are standing—there'd be a Kinko's probably. A lot of footsteps went into that chicken leg you're holding.

Pick Your Locus for Hocus Focus

What is your career fantasy goal? Is it still the same one you created back on Day #1 when we spoke about misdirection? How has it changed as you've been changing along with this book? Decide right now who you really are and what you really want to do. Stop your dilly-dallying and start having some Hocus Focus.

Which reminds me of a good quote:

> *Sure opportunity does knock, but*
> *sometimes you have to go to it, too.*

Just as Colonel Sanders had to knock on 1,009 doors, before he got a bite of interest, you must, too. What is the first door of your fantasy career goal that you must knock on to get what you want? Is it a recording studio, to set up a demo-producing session? Is it a college, to enroll in a class? Is it your Aunt Gladys, who knows someone who knows someone at a company you want to work at? Go knock on this door today.

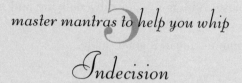

master mantras to help you whip

Indecision

into submission

Next time you feel like you are in a haze and a daze about what to do with your career, remember:

1. I am not a SLAVE who goes back and forth about what I want. I am a MASTER who moves forward.

2. I am not a SLAVE who is wishy-washy about career fantasies. I am a MASTER who has hocus focus.

3. I am not a SLAVE who leaves my career up to the whims of fate. I am a MASTER who takes my career whip in hand and starts a-crackin'.

4. I am not a SLAVE who can't make up my mind. I am a MASTER who makes up my mind—then makes appointments, interviews, and meetings.

5. I am not a SLAVE who is always asking others what I should do. I am a MASTER who asks myself the hard questions, and then listens to myself for the answers.

Whip Workaholism Into Submission

or

Are You Getting Screwed at the Office
and Not at Home?

"If you don't come in on Saturday, don't bother coming in on Sunday" was one of the running jokes in the ad business (or I guess that would be ad busyness?).

I remember there was this one evening that my art director and I got into the elevator to leave at 9 o'clock, and he said to me, "Wow, we got out early tonight." Then we laughed—realizing that 9 o'clock is anything but early to get out. And that's when I realized I really should get out—for good.

Basically I believe:

You must make a life, not just a living.

And, even better, do more living it up.

Hence I am going to quit writing this chapter now and go to the movies.

Just kidding . . .

Though, let me tell you a little bit about your pal, Mistress Karen. Right now I am in my apartment, it's 9:58 P.M., and I am going to be writing until 12 midnight—or until I write another 10 pages—or until I fall asleep in front of my computer, drool dribbling down my chin onto my keyboard, shortcircuiting my computer so it crashes yet again. Though probably that won't happen because I'm on my third cup of coffee.

So what I have learned since my ad days about balance in my life?

Umm . . .

Uh . . .

Hmmm . . .

I have learned something.

1. If you love what you do—which I now do—then working hard doesn't feel as hard on you.
2. I assign myself phone recesses to break up my work, so I can catch up with friends, and stay in the gossip loop. (Otherwise, if I don't watch it, I become the antistalker—someone who *never* calls.)
3. I plan something fun to look forward to when a big work project is complete, to keep me psyched and going—like a concert or a romantic dinner with my paramour.
4. I try to laugh a little each day. I call a funny pal, or read a funny book.
5. I try to love—and be loved—a little each day. I spend time with people who help me keep my arteries healthy and pumping.

6. I try to read a little each day—so I don't become too workcentric or Karencentric—meaning, I stay aware that there is a huge, complicated, populated world pulsating just a few feet away from my office and apartment.
7. I recognize that it's called the "weekend" not the "weakened."
8. If I have to make a little less money to have little more free time, I will. I believe a balanced life is as important as a balanced checkbook.

You Are a Human Being Not a Human Doing

*I*t's important to love what you do, *but you must keep in mind you are more than what you do.* You are who you are when you are just being. Just you. Little old you. Which is really: little young you. The you that you truly are underneath all your defenses and fears and hurts that built up a protective covering around your heart.

Are You Working or Shirking?

*Y*ou might stay at the office later, going over and over a report because you are in avoidance—either about a relationship with someone that isn't working or your relationship with yourself that might not be working. So you might choose to put all your books in alphabetical order, instead of putting in order the role you are now playing with your dysfunctional family.

However, you must know, if you do not spend the time going *within* yourself, you will go *without* something you truly need—like love or the gut-honest answers to the hard questions you have about your parents or spouse. You must pay attention to your real feelings, because respecting your feelings is respecting yourself.

Workaholism Can Be as Bad as Alcoholism

*D*ebbie, an advertising account executive, used to work every night until midnight, and at least ten hours on the weekend. Her husband was always complaining that he never got to see her—that she was married to her job more than she was married to him. Finally, after two years of complaining, Debbie's husband asked for a divorce. Debbie was shocked. Her husband was shocked that Debbie was shocked. He had repeatedly brought up his complaints. But it wasn't until he was out of the door that Debbie saw how her job was preventing her from having true intimacy with her husband. Then she entered therapy and realized she had some major phobias about getting too close to people.

A lot of workaholics relate to Debbie, who now realizes—thanks to therapy—that she used her job as an excuse not to get close to her husband—and her true feelings. "I also realize now that I felt that my *job* was what made me special," says Debbie, "I thought that my success was what made people like me. I had to stop working so hard and get to know who I am—face the parts of me I didn't want to see—and learn to love these parts. I also realize now that I had been lying to myself about how much work I needed to do, so I could avoid the real work I needed to do—working on my feelings and sense of self. I know all this sounds so corny. But I swear, therapy has changed my life. My work life as well as my love life. I now work less hard, but do just as well. And I now I have a new man I'm dating—and I'm very aware of spending enough time with him."

Getting back to the point of this chapter . . .

When Was the Last Time You Had Sex?

*Y*ou can tell me. It's Day #25. We can open up.

Okay, so don't tell me. But tell yourself. And if you haven't been having sex enough lately, do something about it. I know, I know. Sex is not the answer—but it is a fun false start. Seriously, though. Having balance in your life means making sure you keep yourself stimulated in the following ways:

1. Physically.
2. Emotionally.
3. Creatively.
4. Intellectually.
5. Spiritually.

In other words, in between doing your work, you must make sure you have a little bit of the following in working order:

1. Love.
2. Sex.
3. Friendship.
4. Family.
5. Spirituality.
6. Entertainment.
7. Exercise.
8. Travel.

Do you? If not, why not?

Maybe you think that it's not possible. But that's a slave's limited thinking. When you change your idea about what life can be, you can change what your life can be. Remember that 80/20 rule? 80 percent of your results come from 20 percent of your actions. You can find the time. You just have to be disciplined about how you spend your time at the office. IF YOU'RE WORKING HARD TO ACHIEVE SUCCESS, BUT NOT HAVING TIME TO ENJOY YOUR SUCCESS, THEN YOU ARE NOT A SUCCESS.

Or as Christopher Morley said: "There is only one success—to be able to spend your life in your own way."

You know what? With all this in mind, I think I'm going to finish my work up early, cut this chapter short, and do some smooching with my paramour.

See you tomorrow.

Today's Fantasy Role-Playing Exercises
(and Tips for Cracking Whips)

The Mommy Track

*A*lthough I'm not a mom—yet—I recognize how hard it is to juggle work and a baby. But it's—thankfully—becoming easier. So if you've been considering having a baby, but think you don't have the time or money—or do have a baby and are questioning if you have the time or money, then today *do something to research a better way to be both a master mom and a master careerist.* Today look into day care centers near you. Or call up a new nanny service that a friend told you about that you have not called yet. Use the time you've been spending complaining to do something proactive, so you can be the mom of your fantasies as well as have the career of your fantasies.

Are You Crazy About Your Job, or Going Crazy?

*D*o your loved ones complain that they never see you—that any day now they expect to see your photo on the back of a milk carton? If so, maybe you're working too hard. Maybe you need to find out why you're working too hard. Maybe you need to see a therapist—either alone or with your partner. Maybe it wouldn't hurt to try out a few sessions and see if they offer you any clarity. Call a therapist today.

Fear of Commitment: It Could Happen to You—Or Someone You *Can't* Love

Have sex with someone you love today—he'll love you for it . . . and love me for saying this. Trust me. It's good to complain about being an exhausted, sleep-deprived wreck of a human being for other reasons than "I've been working too hard." Or if it's your partner who's working too hard at his job, you can help make your romantic life come alive by calling him today at the office and talking dirty to him—when he can't respond. Just make sure you're not on speakerphone.

Is Your Work Life on the Rocks?

Call information and get the number of your local AA—Alcoholics Anonymous. Ask them to send you a copy of their 12-step program for alcoholism. Wherever there is the word *alcohol* replace it with *work* and read it once again.

Circle the Following

Decide today to make sure you are building a supportive circle of friends. It's important to put in the effort of intimacy with more than just your lifetime partner. So work on leaving work early and spending time with a good friend—preferably a funny friend. I believe the amount you laugh in a day is the true measure of a healthy, balanced person.

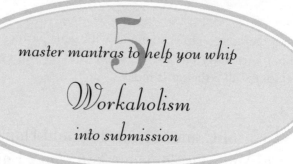

master mantras to help you whip

Workaholism

into submission

Next time you feel your life is all work and no play, remember:

1. I am not a SLAVE who works until the A.M. I am a MASTER who wants to take the time to know WHO I AM.

2. I am not a SLAVE who works round the clock. I am a MASTER who makes the time for the people I love.

3. I am not a SLAVE who thinks here in the nineties you have to work hard to support a family. I am a MASTER who thinks up ways to support a family and still have time for a family.

4. I am not a SLAVE who doesn't know the meaning of *relax.* I am a MASTER who knows that the way to find meaning in my life is to relax.

5. I am not a SLAVE who stays up late and whose world is limited to my office. I am a MASTER who stays up on the world.

Whip

Exhaustion

Into Submission

or

....

Remember: Lethargy Is Not to Be Confused with Calm

....

If the planet Earth didn't already exist, some comedy writer on another planet would have to invent it.

Imagine this wacky planet whose inhabitants can be so rivalous that if they're not competing about who is happier and who has amassed more stuff that either honks or shimmers or is just plain really big, then these inhabitants—now get this funny, comedy-writer spin—are competing to see who is more physically and emotionally exhausted from hard work, who has more low-energy, low-vitality, and has such low get-up-and-go that they can barely move and must thereby have machines take messages for them and other inhabitants on bikes bring them slimy noodles with peanut sauce on top because their job has reduced their brains to an earthling puddle.

We've all been there. We all know. Work can make earthling puddles out of the best of us if we are not careful.

Nancy, a successful TV director, says: "I come home from a day of shooting and cannot move—that's if I'm lucky. Sometimes I start my day like that and I have to shoot for nine hours straight before we take a break."

David, a CEO, says, "I am always feeling like I have to take a nap. But I don't know when to schedule it. Some days I have back-to-back meetings that begin with breakfast at 7 A.M. at the Paramount hotel. Lately in the evening I find I'm even hoarse."

Paul Down the Hall (my neighbor and an advertising creative director) says, "I've been pressing that snooze alarm in the morning about 20 times before I am able to crawl out of bed."

We wear our exhaustion proudly, as if it were some kind of designer garment and we were showing off the high price we had to pay to wear it. "Ooh, aaah," we expect others to say in response to our complaints of low energy. "Boy, you must really have suffered hard at your office to get such an impressive level of fatigue."

But lack of energy is hardly something to be admired in and of itself, and it's certainly not the right state to be in for pushing your career around. The only real way to bring out the passion, energy, vitality, enthusiasm, and vibrancy necessary to succeed in your job is to have the strength to be resilient. As all good dominatrixes of their destinies know: You need be in a turned-on mood to be able to whip a career into a nice submissive state. Remember Principles #11 and #12 of the Master Plan? *"To be a good whipper, you have to keep yourself in a state of excitement."* And: *"You've got to keep whipping and whipping to make a lasting mark."* And remember Mistress Karen's other ofttimes-repeated-usually-in-*italicized-type*-to-get-your-attention-and-here-we-go-yet-again-my-S&M-that's-success-and-money-career philosophy:

To master your outer world, you must first master your inner world. When you can master your thoughts, you can master your mood, your energy, your life.

3 Down, Only 59,997 Left to Go

I mentioned earlier that brain researchers say that we have about 60,000 thoughts a day. As a master of your destiny you can—through conscious discipline—choose *not* to make too many of those 60,000 be too negative. For instance: "I hate this assignment! I hate this job! I hate this little weasel of a life I'm living!" are three thoughts you might want to strike from your repertoire.

It's like this: Your brain has 100 billion cells—each of these little babies is connected to at least 20,000 other cells. The variety of potential combinations of all of these are more multitudinous than the number of molecules that exist in all of the universe! What this means is: If you have *that* many different combinations of brain cells to choose from, then why not try a new combo today? Come on. You can do it. You have literally over a billion combinations to choose from that could be more beneficial to your well-being that going with the standard: "Just shoot me now" thought bubble that is all too often hovering over your head.

In the movie *Annie Hall,* Woody Allen's character gets physically ill and emotionally feeble when he has to give a speech. He hates presenting in front of large groups, so he's worked himself into a state of lethargy. When the speech is canceled suddenly Woody is full of vim and vigor.

In other words, when he was operating under Slave Mentality—torturing himself with fear, weakening himself with doubt—his energy and health sank low. When he was able to unshackle the fears and doubts that held him down, he rose back up to a good spirit zone.

Nancy, the TV director, confesses, "Sometimes I'll be really tired before a shoot and someone will compliment me on something they saw that I directed and I'll feel an automatic energy boost."

David, that CEO, also admits, "I can feel as if I cannot take another step and—this is embarrassing to admit, but what the hell—then I'll see a beautiful woman in the conference room and my energy will suddenly get a lift. And just so you don't think I'm a total cad, I also find that after a really great meeting my energy level comes back up on the charts again."

Hey, Whatever Turns You On

The trick is to find the thing that turns you on, and use it when you need that energy lift most. And another trick of the master trade:

You must acknowledge that important philosophical concept: "Hey, shit happens."

Sometimes it's one particular horrific assignment that lets the air out of your energy pack. Maybe you just found out a project you were excited about was canceled or someone else got the promotion you wanted. Whatever. You're bummed and feeling earth puddlesque—yet you have a huge assignment due. What now? You can barely move.

As a master of your destiny you must master your thoughts so you're not centered in on the "bad"—and muster your energy to move forward toward the good you need to create. After all, who you really are is most truly revealed by how you are able to handle yourself and your responsibilities when you are under pressure—whether or not you love that David Bowie song "Under Pressure"—which I think is a very cool tune . . . *mmmm, under pressure.* I'm singing it now. Come on. Why don't you join in with me: *mmmm, under pressure . . . mmmm, under pressure.* You gotta love that song.

Speaking of Singing

$\mathcal{M}$y neighbor Paul Down the Hall, the creative director, says: "When I'm really feeling low energy, I put on my Walkman and blast some good music. I just got the soundtrack to *The Full Monty* and listened to it before a client presentation the other day. It totally pumped me up."

You, too, must create your own personalized strategy to rile yourself back up into a feverish energy frenzy next time you feel stupordom strike. Just as a football coach knows what to say to a weary, injured team to get them full of fighting spirit, you must talk to yourself within your own head this way. You must direct all your energy and efforts into one definite purpose: *Win whatever you're fighting for.* That may be a report, a client, a new position. Know: *You have the potential inside you to master anything you want—and muster the energy to do it.*

Whenever I'm feeling lack of energy to do another ounce of work, I indulge in the following "Four Play" to get me turned back on again.

Mistress Karen's Four Play to Turn You On

1. Remember what you have in your career that you are already excited about. For me it's: I love being able to write a screenplay that will make people giggle—and think. For you it might be: I love working with smart, talented people who challenge me to be the best business person I can be.
2. Remember how you got it. For me it's: I almost gave up my film fantasies, then my film guardian angel, Marisa Tomei, came through. For you it might be: I started off as a junior person in the company and have risen up by repeatedly proving myself as a unique thinker.

3. Let these memories of achievement dominate your mind.

4. Demand this same positivity from yourself to do the work that's on your desk.

Where There's a Wail There's a Way

Sometimes—although you might not want to admit it—we enjoy our lethargy because it's our intuitive way to get a little reassurance or nurturing or attention from others. Could these be some of the reasons that you've been complaining to others about your low energy level? Maybe you just need a little lovin'. If so, show some "wailpower" over your complaining and try an alternative route. My recommendation: Directly ask for these emotional needs from those you love whom you want love back from.

Or maybe you need to ask for these tender loving feelings back from your job. . . .

Is the Honeymoon Over Between You and Your Job?

Maybe you and your job have been seeing too much of each other and you forgot what you love about each other. Maybe you need to do something different to put the sparks back into your love affair with your work. Like perhaps you need to set higher goals for yourself to get yourself psyched to go into the office. *Ironically sometimes we get tired when a job is too easy rather than when a job is too hard.* Challenges can supply an extra energy boost.

Or Maybe You Just Need to Take a Vacation From Your Vocation

Another way to RENEW YOUR PASSION for your work is to take a break away from it so you can remember what you loved about it in the first place. Sometimes this distance can help you see how far you've come in your career and appreciate it and yourself a bit more. When you return to your job you'll return more turned-on than ever to take on more than ever. Or sometimes this distance can help you see specific problems and complaints that you didn't know you had that are bringing you down (for instance, maybe you need to ask for an assistant because you're doing too much minutia work, or maybe you need to fire your assistant because you realize she's snippy instead of snappy about doing the work she needs to do). If so, be sure when you get back to the office you do something about these problems and complaints—besides just complaining. Maybe you'll be tempted to EXPLORE SOME NEW, EXCITING POSITIONS within your company that could turn you on more than your present position.

The Girlfriend Board

We women in particular have to watch out for the dangers of complaining. I have what I call *The Girlfriend Board*—a group of supportive girlfriends who help one another out by sharing our problems. Women tend to do this with one another more than men because we value intimacy and bonding more, and fear being vulnerable less. The problem is that sometimes when we talk about every nook and cranny of our psyches, we expand our opportunity for getting truly bummed out—and thereby lethargic. Sometimes we don't even notice that these conversations are 90 percent complaint sessions and only 10 percent pep talk. I must admit, if I don't watch it, I can find myself launching into a Woody Allenesque self-deprecatory existential crisis mode, not even caring about the positive advice waiting for me on the other side. For me it's sometimes fun to just complain. But then again: I am a humorist. This is my job. My best funny anecdotes are centered around complaining about stuff, not about how perfect life is. Perfect lives don't sell as well to publishers and Hollywood.

But if you're not in the business of exposing your tragedy for the world to laugh at, there really aren't any big advantages to complaining *all the time* and getting yourself bummed out and lethargic—at least none I can think of. So, I say—*cut it out.*

It's up to you to move past self-pitying exhaustion and make things happen, instead of complaining about things that happen. Through conscious thought you can bring yourself back up to high energy levels and thereby higher levels of work. Through conscious thought you can perk up and enjoy this present moment—like this one right now.

Be Happy and Peppy Right Now, Right Where You Are

Stop waiting for specific things to happen to become happy and vital and full of passion for living. Stop waiting for life to begin. It has begun. The starter gun has been shot—and unless it's hit you in the tush, there's no reason you shouldn't be moving giddily forward—right this moment. Get going! SCRAM! I mean it! What are you waiting for?

Today's Fantasy Role-Playing Exercises
(and Tips for Cracking Whips)

Power Pact

When I was a dieting teenager, I used to tape up photos of skinny gorgeous girls on the walls of my refrigerator. It inspired me to lose weight. Although my brother Eric gained about ten pounds. Find Power Photos from your own life of times you won awards—or any photo in a magazine of some Power Babe or Power Dude that inspires you and psyches you up to be coolest master of the career universe.

Unfrozen Yoga

Today make an appointment to check out some yoga. It will not only show you how to make your body less stiff and more flexible, over time it will make your attitude about problems feel less stiff and your approach to solving them more limber.

Skeptic Tank

Sometimes we're worried about stuff we aren't aware of and it's creating a sludge in our energy flow. For instance, maybe you have an overly full skeptic tank right now. What things at the office keep you skeptical about success? Write them down. Now write down reasons to be psyched about these worries and not worry so much.

Get Trigger Happy

*B*estselling author and motivational speaker Tony Robbins believes that sometimes what causes you to get bummed is something you unconsciously see that triggers unhappy memories. So become a detective. Do you have any objects or photos around your office that remind you of unhappy times—like stuff representative of a painful divorce or a motorcycle accident or a person you loathe? If so, trash it.

master mantras to help you whip

Exhaustion

into submission

Next time you're so tired you wanna retire, remember:

1. I am not a SLAVE who gets bogged down by bad thoughts. I am a MASTER who wants things so badly I never allow myself to feel badly.

2. I am not a SLAVE who thinks being tired is impressive. I am a MASTER who thinks being retired after a successful career is impressive.

3. I am not a SLAVE who has lost the will to even get up to get another cup of coffee. I am a MASTER who zips around the office without the aid of coffee—well, at least not more than two cups.

4. I am not a SLAVE who gets turned on by complaining. I am a MASTER who gets turned on by doing.

5. I am not a SLAVE who lives in a tense future tense. I am a MASTER who knows how to relax and enjoy the ride—and maybe an occasional shiatsu.

Whip

Learning

Into Submission

or

....

Experience Is a Good Teacher—
but So Are Books, Magazines, and Classes

....

One of my career big breaks in my career came because I was reading dog training manuals looking for tips to teach my cat a few tricks. (Note: I really wanted a dog. My building doesn't allow them. Dogs bark. Cats don't. So I got a cat and tried to raise it to be a dog. I was hoping that, in the same way parents who were rooting for a son and got a daughter, might wind up with a girl who grew up to be a tomboy, that my cat might become a tomdog.)

So there I was reading this manual and I realized that many of the tips not only applied to both dogs and cats alike, but men, too. (For instance, flight and chase behavior. Dog trainers say that if your dog is running away from you the worst thing to do is to chase after him, because that will only make him run away faster.) My amusement soon transformed itself into what would soon become a bestselling book: *How To Make Your Man Behave in 21 Days or Less Using the Secrets of Professional Dog Trainers*. The lesson to master?

You Never Know Where Career Inspiration Will Come From

*I*n the movie *Working Girl*, Melanie Griffith plays a secretary who gets a visionary idea for her company one morning over her low-fat banana muffin and the morning paper—from the gossip column, no less. Great ideas can come from all kinds of reading: books, newspapers, magazines, bumper stickers, tattoos. Hence, it's important to read a little every day, because:

The person with the widest range of knowledge is destined to become the person with the most career luck.

And to show that I live up to my "read stuff daily" philosophy of living, here's a quote from John Kenneth Galbraith I just read yesterday:

"Money is what fueled the industrial society. But in the informational society, the fuel, the power, is knowledge. One has now come to see a new class structure divided by those who have information and those who must function out of ignorance. This new class has its power not from money, not from land, but from knowledge."

In other words . . . get on the Internet, buddy! The new haves and have-nots are the Internet-savvy and Internet-savvy-nots. So power up and get the power that knowledge—as it's rumored to have—truly offers.

Yes, Knowledge Is Indeed Power

And the opposite is true, too. Ignorance breeds powerlessness—because it breeds fear. The less you know, the more you have to fear messing up or saying something Neanderthalesque or being power-played by someone with more knowledge than you. A master of one's destiny thereby strives to get whip smart, by developing a deep belly hunger for knowledge—and feeding it brain food, not junk food. So, voilà. Here's the Zagat's guide to your brain zygotes:

Nine Recommended Locations
That Serve Brain Food

1. *College.* It's never too late to learn. In fact, classes can start as late as 9:30 in the evening! So there are no excuses not to further your education. Many a master of one's destiny decides to go for a master in sociology, psychology, screenwriting—whatever it takes to give a new career a try or an existing career a facelift. This can also include just interesting classes at your local Learning Annex on wine tasting, so you not only have good wine to serve guests in your home, but good party patter to offer at business functions.

2. *Experience on the job.* It's not enough to do good work, you must strive to do consistently better and better work. Decide to become absolutely excellent at the thing you do by refining your craft until it reaches connoisseur levels—and success will follow you like a stalker.

3. *Others who are experts.* Just as you can improve your tennis game by playing with a better opponent, you can improve your career by hanging around people who are more successful than you, then asking them what their big break was, what their best business tip is, and if they see anything in your career life they would suggest you change.

4. *Others who just know stuff.* Every person is a potential teacher. For instance, George Clooney would make a fine sex ed

teacher, if you ask me. But seriously . . . Some of the most un-suspecting people you meet might be able to teach you some-thing. Your taxi driver. Your secretary. Your employee. (Even—surprise, surprise—your boss!) Be open to receiving knowledge from all sources.

5. *Libraries/bookstores.* All the answers to any of the ques-tions you can fathom can be found in books. Others have made the same mistakes you've made—or are about to make—and they write down all their humiliating lessons in books and mem-oirs to help protect you from being the idiot they were. For in-stance, *The Seven Habits of Highly Effective People;* any of the *Chicken Soup for the Soul* series; and *Smart Women, Foolish Choices: Stupid Things Women Do To Mess Up Their Lives.* Plus check out the biographies of Benjamin Franklin, Coco Chanel, and Ayn Rand.

6. *Magazines and newspapers.* It's important to stay current on trends and stay aware of opinions you did not even know you had until someone pissed you off in an article. I like to read ar-ticles by people I think I'll disagree with—like editorials that are antiabortion or pro–capital punishment—so I can really under-stand myself and why I hold my own views all the more.

7. *Special outside interest classes.* You must be more than you do. Develop a wide sphere of interests and skills so that next time you are at a business function—or cocktail party—you don't just have to talk your line of work. You can be well rounded.

8. *Trade publications, gossip rags.* Know thy target audi-ence—and well—so you can be sure you're digging where the gold is.

9. *Group brainstorming/think tanks.* Often it pays to work with a couple of someones you feel are mentally challenging thinkers. You can create original synergy together. I remember reading in *The Lives of a Cell* that a termite alone cannot fly— it needs the energy of another termite near it to be able to flutter its wings. Same goes for people. Sometimes you just need the en-ergy of others to get an idea off the ground. So consider forming your own Algonquin table of debate.

Brainpower Is as Important as Horsepower

*I*t's not enough just to do your job. You must do your job with conscious thought—master your skill to its peak level—and know that success not only requires hard work, but hard, hard, hard work. And that means learning everything you can about BOTH the project you're doing AND the client you're doing it for. Meaning:

Research. Research. Research.

Read up. Read up. Read up.

For instance, when *Playboy* magazine wanted me to write an article reporting on which condoms were the most "natural" feeling, my boyfriend and I worked long and hard—pulling all-nighters, researching and researching and re-researching—devoted researchers that we were.

You must do the same for your career. If you're working for a Hong Kong–based company, learn all about Hong Kong. If you're presenting lingerie concepts to a variety of department store buyers, learn everything about the lingerie fabrics you are using and each department store buyer you are selling to—*before you go into the meeting*. And never—ever, ever—go into a meeting unprepared. There's an old expression:

Do a great job, three people will find out.
Do a horrible job, everyone will find out.

So, if you can't do it with excellence, don't do it at all. And if you *can*—it's payback time, because people pay extra for quality work. The more quality work you have to offer, the more likely you are to have lucky breaks. So decide today to be the best at your job—whatever that takes.

For instance . . . Gina started out making her own home-made small films with a video camera. A friend of hers showed Gina's films to a friend who showed them to a friend over at

MTV. Next thing Gina knew, she was hired to direct and produce promos.

Which was both great news and a big problem—because Gina was not fully educated in film production.

You Must Stop Talking About Problems and Start Researching Solutions

*G*ina could have had a Slave Mentality about taking on a job before she was ready—meaning she could have risked being pushed around by others who saw her weakness—or neurotically worried daily to friends that she was messing up. But Gina took her career whip in hand and whipped her lack of education before it whipped her. Rather than risk falling on her face at the job, Gina quickly took a film class at NYU on the side, and cross-examined all her film-savvy buddies on everything they knew about directing/producing the coolest work possible.

In the end, Gina not only displayed her talent as a film director but her talent as a dominatrix of her destiny, by showing she had two of the two essential things you need to succeed:

Great Aptitude + Great Attitude

Today's Fantasy Role-Playing Exercises
(and Tips for Cracking Whips)

There's a Difference Between Knowing and Doing

*I*t's not enough to learn stuff. You've got know how to ap- ply what you learn to your work. For instance, Melanie Griffith's character might have read that article in the paper, but not done anything with her idea. Is there some inspiration you recently had from reading something that you have done noth- ing about yet? If so, go out there and do something about it today. As Thomas Henry Huxley said: "The great end of life is not knowledge but action."

If You Love It, Then Learn It

*I*s there some interest you've had that you keep threatening to take a class in but have yet to live up to your threats? If so, don't delay. Call up some nearby schools and get a catalog. Then sign up—or shut up.

Read My Clips

*S*tart a folder of your favorite articles that you stumble upon when reading. You never know when they'll come in handy at the office.

Master Class

Sometimes the best way to master something is by teaching that something. My friend Susan teaches comedy writing—and has improved her craft in the process, by constantly being reminded what works—and doesn't work—by reading her students' work.

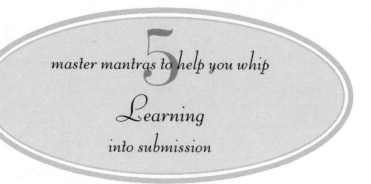

master mantras to help you whip

5

Learning

into submission

Next time you feel you're not in the mood to strain your lil' brain, remember:

1. I am not a SLAVE who restrains myself with limited thinking. I am a MASTER who retrains myself to see unlimited opportunity

2. I am not a SLAVE who hears "No way." I am a MASTER who hears "Know the way."

3. I am not a SLAVE who says, "I don't have time to take a class." I am a MASTER who finds the time for learning—knowing this time now will equal money later.

4. I am not a SLAVE who holds myself back by not expanding outside my job. I am a MASTER who loves what I do—as well as loves learning.

5. I am not a SLAVE who hears, "Sorry, no more job openings." I am a MASTER who hears, "If I know more—go back to school—there will be more job opportunities."

Whip
People Skills
Into Submission

or

....

Whatever Business You Are in,
You Are in the People Business

....

ot many people know this about me, but sometimes I have a Talking Barbie doll arrange my business meetings for me.

Go ahead. Blink and read that again.

It's true.

One of my clients, Scott, a senior VP at Nickelodeon, got me Barbs as a gift one day while we were in Toys R Us looking at kids' toys and talking about trends in children's TV programming. Afterward, whenever I would call Scott and he wouldn't be in, I'd let Talking Barbie leave a message for me on his voicemail. Usually she says something like: "Let's go to the mall with Midge and have pizza." But Scott knows that's Barb's code for, "Let's go to the Paramount with Karen and talk about doing work together."

People Love People Who Love Goofiness

*H*aving a warped sense of humor has helped not only my writing career, but my people bonding career—gave it super glue power. People love to laugh and have fun during a grumble-grumble-must-we-work-why-can't-we-all-have-trust-funds work day. I always try to supply a little humor and good cheer along with whatever work is due.

Lee, owner/director of Lee Hunt Associates, also recognizes the importance of humor in the workplace. His office is staffed with folks who could be backup writers for David Letterman. That's one of the reasons I love working with Lee. Plus his people skills repertoire also includes having ample trust in those he works with.

Although Lee never got me a Talking Barbie, he did get me talking to NBC and CBS. Whenever he was overflowing with work, he'd refer his clients to me, trusting I wouldn't permanently lure them away—and I showed my loyalty by not.

The epilogue?

It's been over nine years since we started working together and Lee and I are *still working together.* I love the guy.

Actually ALL of Lee's staff loves the guy—because he knows how to lead by example, treat them the way he wants to be treated—and the way he treats himself.

Your Example Speaks More Loudly Than Anything You Can Say

*Y*ou as a master must first be who you want others to think you are. Meaning? If you want to have peaceful relations with others, you must first make peace with your character flaws—uh, make that your "character eccentricities." If you have a temper, temper it. If you are undependable, become un-

undependable. Build your image as strong, competent, disciplined, decent, balanced. Master your character, instead of being a slave to your weaknesses. Place the fantasy of who you want to be and how you want others to treat you in the front burner of your mind. According to the law of attraction, you will attract these qualities and attitudes to you over time—or your head will burst into flames. It's one or the other. I forget which. But I think it's worth taking the risk to find out.

Be a Dyslexic Paranoid—Suspect Everyone of Secretly Plotting to Make you Giddily Happy

The big number one secret to being good with people is to basically love people. I am a people person. I am sincerely curious about people, and what motivates them. For instance, in the coffee shop I go to every morning, I always see interesting characters. I wonder about the life of the little old lady who on Mondays is always circling her week's pick in *TV Guide* with a large purple marker. And who is that guy with the beret and large golden retriever who buys Evian water for his dog to drink while he sips his cappuccino? This is what I love about writing screenplays and novels—the opportunity to explore how and why people do the things they do.

Focus on Being Interested, Rather Than Worry About Being Interesting

Tony Robbins suggests that a good way to bond with people is to ask them when was the last time they were truly motivated and passionate about something or someone. Then he listens to the ingredients they list (like fine Italian leather shoes or, say, maybe, virgin sacrificial offerings), and he works them into his recipe for dealing with them in the future ("Have I got a virgin for you!"). Robbins also suggests figuring out if they're verbal people or visual people. If they're more visually inclined, he uses visual aids to get them going in a business meeting—even purposefully uses visually oriented language like "I *see* what you mean." "It *appears* to *look* that way." He believes you can subconsciously bond more strongly with a visual person this way. If they're verbal, apply good, strong vocabulary usage.

A Master Knows How to Make Others Feel Like a Master

Another good bondage—oops, I mean bonding—technique is to always show your appreciation for what makes a person unique—then express your high regard for these qualities to them. Obviously you must flatter with sincerity behind your compliments, or your flattery will go flat. For instance, if someone "um-ed" and "ah-ed" all the way through a presentation, even knocking down the microphone by flailing his hands around as he talked, do *not* tell him that he is a great public speaker. This is *not* the way to create a new friend, but a person who will be suspicious of everything you say from then on. Instead you should make him feel better about his presentation by reassuring him about the positive parts. Compliment him on how detailed the research was within the work presented. Compliment him on his bravery to present to such a large, intimidating group. It's not hard to find qualities to respect in someone—even a dinkhead. (Even Hitler had an adoring *Fraulein* on the side.)

The most important thing is *not* to walk around thinking:

People suck.

Even if people do sometimes suck, you should try to figure out the why behind the sucking noise they emit.

Elaine, a marketing executive, says: "I had this one coworker who snarled at me one morning at the coffee machine. I didn't want to deal with her after that. Then someone at my office revealed to me that this person's mother had just been hospitalized the day before. I felt really bad about my quick assessment and immediately went up to her and offered my warmest hopes for a fast recovery."

A Master of One's Destiny Recognizes Other People Have Destinies, Too—and Sometimes These Destinies Have Bad Stuff That Can Create Temporary Bad Moods

It's important to remain open to understanding why people act like goofballs sometimes, rather than just shutting a door in their faces.

Fran, a social worker, says, "I always tell my clients that the world is their mirror. If someone is always yelling at them at the office, they shouldn't just strictly view this person as an evil shmuck. They should look at themselves, their behavior, and how they might have contributed to the problem. I believe that sometimes even a shmuck can teach you things, even if their teaching presentation is wrong."

You're Only as Good with Others as You Are with Yourself

*B*asically you should treat others the way you want to be treated. And this means if they're bugging you, talk openly to them about it (see my chapter on communication for more tips on this). You must make a commitment to wanting to develop loving relationships with the people in your life. Because I believe, basically, the only thing you can never have too much of is love—oh, and shoes.

If you want to find some good long-lasting shoes, check out Tootsi Ploughhound in Manhattan, New York, on 20th and Fifth Avenue.

If you want to find some good long-lasting people relationships, check out the following list:

Mistress Karen's Tips for Cracking That Whip at Long-Lasting, Loving Work Relationships

1. Be the most positive person you know. You'll attract people like cat hair to velvet—and in time like cat hair to a cat.
2. Keep conversations short. Don't waste people's time.
3. Know who is good to talk to for what. Don't see all people as appropriate to talk to about all things. (For instance, you wouldn't ask a virgin for sex tips, and you wouldn't ask a floundering, unsuccessful accountant how to be a prosperous accountant—though if he looks like George Clooney, you might want to ask him for sex tips).
4. Think of people who inspire you, and seek them out. Through osmosis you'll benefit from knowing them.

5. Keep a certain mystique; don't be a billboard for your own insecurities.

6. Avoid gossip. Hurt can hurt people. When you go spilling beans all over the place, you only make a mess of yourself in the end.

7. Be sincerely interested in others. Ask questions. Then actually listen to responses. And remember those responses later on.

8. Value humor.

9. Show grace and strong character under fire.

10. Know family matters matter. Don't let work keep you away from your loved ones when they need you.

11. Guard your time so you can satisfy your interests and yourself—but don't be self-centered.

12. Show forgiveness. And even bother to show it out loud. Apologize when appropriate.

13. Overlook petty weaknesses (someone who is always five minutes late, or who keeps a messy office). When you're focused on flaws, you find them everywhere. When you focus on the good . . . you get the good stuff.

14. Be kind, but not a slavish wimp.

15. Be aware of the essence of people—like in poker game, look for "tells."

16. Recognize that sometimes even a shmuck can teach you things.

17. Perform small kind, gestures. Like on birthdays, send a small gift.

18. Tackle your own "character eccentricities" (aka weaknesses) daily.

19. Be humble. Don't brag.

20. Be serene.

21. Give more than you receive. In both work time and emotional feedback.

22. Live honorably and truthfully.

23. Be patient. Battle your "wait" problem as best as you can.
24. Be generous.
25. Be on time.
26. Share your knowledge.
27. Say thank you—often.

Familiarize yourself with the above. Once you've got it down, then get it up to give it all to people daily—then add more people to your daily people encounters.

One of the big secrets to success—which is not much of a secret—is to keep up with your networking. And keep in mind that every person you meet offers the potential to meet five more people!

So make it a daily habit to talk to new people. Wait. Let me rephrase that—to *listen* to new people.

Today's Fantasy Role-Playing Exercises
(and Tips for Cracking Whips)

Learn from Your Mentors—
Instead of Tormentors

rite down the names of people you most admire, then list next to each the qualities about them you admire most. For instance: honest, organized, impishly charismatic. Pick three qualities that you will work on at work. Also, pick up the phone and plan some activities with your mentors so you can, through osmosis, benefit from their charms. Go to a museum, golfing—do whatever people in your industry are into.

Go to a Place No Man Has Ever Been Before— Explore Inner Space

*T*o be your best you need to know who you are and why you think the way you do. So make a list of your ten worst "character eccentricities." Today vow to try to correct these.

Is Your Ego an Estop?

*A*re you too stuck on yourself to pay loving attention to others? Today try to have a lot of conversations with people without saying "I."

Are You in a Bad Relation-*shit*— Oops, I Mean Relationship?

*I*n your journal write down the names of people who are big-time in your life: business associates, your spouse, a best friend, your mother, your father, any kids, neighbors. Now write down next to each how you feel you could improve your relationships with these people in the next year.

master mantras to help you whip

People Skills

into submission

Next time you feel you're into researching people killing instead of people skills, remember:

1. I am not a SLAVE who walks around feeling bitter about people. I am a MASTER who tries to better understand people.

2. I am not a SLAVE who talks nonstop. I am a MASTER who listens nonstop.

3. I am not a SLAVE who says, "I can't help myself. I've always been this way." I am a MASTER who says, "How can I help myself become a high-quality human?"

4. I am not a SLAVE who says, "A shmuck is a shmuck is a shmuck." I am a master who says, "For every shmuck there is the shmuckee. What shmuck-bait did I perhaps put out to attract this behavior?"

5. I am not a SLAVE who is always rapping people on the knuckles for every little thing they do. I am a MASTER who establishes rapport.

Whip
Stress
Into Submission

or

....

Be Pro-Process and Not Pro-Stress

....

I think there should be a new flavor of Ben and Jerry's ice cream called "Deadline Crunch Crazy." Whenever I'm completely stressed out about a project that's due, like, say, in an hour—like, say, the book you are working on (just to let you in on a peek of Mistress Karen's life there for a moment)—well, I suddenly develop quite a hearty lil' appetite.

Although many might argue that eating sugary substances while stressed out of one's mind might not be the most appropriate panacea—I find that having a new thing to be stressed out about, like uh-oh, I shouldn't have eaten that, I think I just gained ten pounds—well, this helps to distract me from my original stress so I can get my project (like this book) completed.

Even though I am joking, I am serious. (Although I'm always serious—except when I'm joking.) I *do* believe that although ice cream might not be the exact way to go about pursuing a diversion, a good technique to cut down on stress is to divert oneself.

A Stress Distraction Leads to Stress Subtraction

*F*or example, consider the following true (and humiliating) story:

A True and Humiliating Story

I was taking a break one Saturday morning from finishing a substantial section of this very book—that was due to my editor on Monday morning—when I looked over at my computer and it looked back at me blankly.

Literally blankly.

It had (surprise, surprise) crashed again.

I was supposed to meet my friend Bryan for coffee in three minutes.

At first I decided to skip coffee and go directly to the computer repair store (maybe killing a few small children and some puppies on the way). Ultimately, I met Bryan at the cafe and told him what happened. He smiled and took one of his large hands, messed up my hair and in a goofy voice said, "You've done it again!" and laughed in a jokey, maniacal way to try to get me to relax and laugh at myself.

It worked.

"Hey, getting stressed out won't fix the computer," Bryan reminded me. "Besides, nowadays they can fix anything that goes wrong with a computer," he generously lied.

Then as we walked over to the computer store he teased me about what I was wearing because it was low cut. (Hey, I'm not called Mistress Karen for nothing.) I buttoned up my sweater to create a nun neckline instead of a fun neckline. And merrily into the computer repair store we went—only to be shot down.

"We don't repair computers over the weekend. We can only get to it on Monday," said Sing, the repair guy.

Because Bryan had put me in such a playful mood, I found myself responding with: "So . . . what's your store policy on bribery? Could I convince you to look at it now?"

Sing smiled.

"Oh wait, I forgot I'm wearing something low cut. Does this help to convince you?" I asked, then unbuttoned my sweater and gave him a pique peek (at my peaks, so to speak—I'm sorry about that bad humor. Obviously the stress got to me.).

Next thing I knew Sing was unzippering . . . (I don't know what you're thinking right now, but I'm about to say "my computer case") . . . my computer case (see, I told you that's all I was about to say! Hmph!).

I'm still not sure if it was my humor or my cleavage, but the next thing I knew, Sing was helping me fix my broken computer.

Guess what?

It wasn't even broken! It had merely become unplugged overnight and the battery had gone dead!

The computer worked just fine and dandy.

That's when I did a little two-step-four-step-my-computer-hard-drive-is-saved dance for joy, which is not to be confused with my friend Terri's my-divorce-is-final jig of happiness.

The Lesson on Stressin'?

1. Because I was already stressed from being in deadline hell, I could only see the blank screen from a stressful person's viewpoint of horror. My mind could not be relaxed and receptive to be open to other happier explanations.

2. Plus, I was associating *past stress* with a innocent present situation—having experienced my Technology Mary epidemic of broken computers.

3. When Bryan relaxed me, I entered into a stress-free state that allowed me to handle people in such a way that they were open to helping me, thereby solving my problem.
4. The moral? Next time you're stressed, you should all call Bryan. His unlisted home phone number is 555–1212. Just kidding. We should all get in touch with our "Inner Bryan"—that more jovial spirit inside of us that helps us see the joke during stress—instead of the yoke of doom.

In the book *Demian*, Hermann Hesse writes that fate and temperament are basically the same word. The mood in which you approach a situation can definitely affect its outcome.

My brother, Eric, a stockbroker, says, "When there are severe fluctuations in the market, I advise clients not to make decisions from stress, either bad or good stress—for instance, if they've suddenly made millions. Instead, they should relax, and from this place of calm decide what to do. Always operate from strength not weakness."

Basically, what Eric, Hermann Hesse, Bryan, Sing, and I are all cashing in on are the benefits that come when you are not living in a tense-future-tense, or a projected-negative-tense-past, but rather living fully and calmly in the present moment.

Remember that TV show *Bewitched?* The way magic could happen was by "pausing time." Samantha would freeze the world around her, do her witchcraft thing, then unfreeze the world and watch good things unfold. You, too, can learn to work this magic of "pausing time" by re-learning how to be fully present—and then getting the magical benefits of clear thinking and good judgment and a workable—damn adorable—computer.

Mistress Karen's Five Tips for Whipping Yourself Into the Present Tense

1. Acupuncture.
2. Yoga.
3. Meditation.
4. Workouts at the gym.
5. Breathing exercises.

Listen to Mistress Karen. I know what I'm talking about. After all, do you see that word "mistress"? Look closely . . . see how it has the words "mi *stress*" in it? You know what that means? It means I've been writing too much and I am stressed out and need to take a break because that kind of minutia noting is the thinking of a crazy person.

So maybe you should listen to Jonathan instead.

Jonathan, an award-winning documentary filmmaker, says, "I recognize that stress is part of the cycle of life, and I try to embrace it, channel it to my benefit. For instance, when I went to pitch my movie *The Farm* to a room full of European backers, I was nervous knowing that I was the first American to pitch to the European market. My mind suddenly froze. I couldn't get out of that robotic cycle. Then I realized all that stress was energy in my gut—lots of energy. So I started to use an inner chant, telling myself it was positive energy to be channeled in my pitch. I consciously turned my fear energy into courage energy. When it was time for me to talk, I went right from that place of tension, and finished what was supposed to be a five-minute pitch in only two and half minutes. Next thing I knew I heard everyone clapping—and I got my funding."

Jonathan has since gone on to win the Grand Jury prize for this film—*The Farm*—at the Sundance Film Festival.

Margaret, a cake designer, also admits to bouts of stress. "Whenever I'm stressed, I cut back on the cigarettes and coffee," says Margaret. "I know that those are two 'duh's.' But I often avoid doing the obvious."

Some other "duh-level-obvious" stress reducers include: Cutting back on the alcohol, eating a hearty breakfast, sleeping about seven to eight hours, working under ten hours, and avoiding sugar.

Plus it helps to stay clear from computers—oh, and it helps not to be Jewish. Just trust me on this last one.

Today's Fantasy Role Playing Exercises
(and Tips For Cracking Whips)

Pressure Points

*T*oday is as good a day as any to get naked with a stranger who has firm fingers and a Germanic accent. In other words, schedule a massage. If you live in New York, check out Antje at Casa de Vida in Manhattan, 212-673-2272.

Coffee, Tea, or Valium?

*D*on't drink anything with caffeine in it today—or the next week, if you can. Note how different you feel and decide if your love for java is worth all the extra stress that caffeine can bring.

Human Hurricanes

*T*here are certain people who bring out the stress monster inside of us. I'll tell you who mine are if you'll tell me yours. Write your list, then vow to keep away from these people, especially during high stress times. After all, this is why God created caller ID. If you don't have it at your office yet, demand they get it soon.

Do You Have This Stress in a Smaller Size?

When do you feel most stressed? Is there a certain time of day? Or after certain foods? For the next seventy-two hours, keep a stress diary to see if you can sense a pattern.

Punch and Moody

Invest in a punching bag—or hit your local gym to find one to hit. You'll find that after a passionate round of punching, you'll be ready to hit that pile of work again.

master mantras *5* help you whip

Stress

into submission

Next time you feel you're ready to quit your stressful present job and pursue a career as a serial killer, remember . . .

1. I am not a SLAVE who freaks out at the slightest problem. I am a MASTER who seeks out the answer to all problems.

2. I am not a SLAVE who guzzles coffee by the keg. I am a MASTER who learns how to say "I'll have a decaf, please."

3. I am not a SLAVE who doesn't find time to exercise. I am a MASTER who exercises good judgment in my schedule so I find time to exercise.

4. I am not a SLAVE who thinks being anxious all the time is the only way to live. I am a MASTER who knows how to relax to the max.

5. I am not a SLAVE who can't sleep. I am a MASTER who—rest assured—sleeps seven hours minimum nightly.

Heavy Breather,

the Sequel

or

....

So, Was It as Good for You as It Was for Me?

....

It's day thirty and I want to know:

Did you have a good time? Were you stimulated? Did you reach climaxes of thought you believed could only be achieved with another live human being and not some mere printed words on a page? Are you a changed man—or a changed woman—or so changed that you're now a man who is a woman?

Let's get back on that scale of one through ten and weigh in. Rate yourself—as you did on Day #15—in all of the following areas:

MISDIRECTION	REGRET
FEAR	ANGER
CYNICISM	WORRY

BAD MOOD   GUILT
BLAME   CRAZY DAY
IMPATIENCE   JEALOUSY
PROCRASTINATION   CHANGE
LISTENING   INTUITION
HEALTH   INDECISION
EARNINGS   WORKAHOLISM
DELEGATION   EXHAUSTION
PERFECTIONISM   LEARNING
MEANINGLESSNESS   PEOPLE SKILLS
COMMUNICATION   STRESS

As you hopefully remember from your last Heavy Breather Day, Mistress Karen wants you to rate your progress on the above list in the following ways:

1. Your level of day-to-day change in behavior when it comes to each daily subject.
2. Your level of long-term change in your career progression when it comes to each daily subject (in other words, have these lessons helped you move forward closer to your goal?)
3. Your level of how others have noticed a change in you when it comes to each daily subject.
4. Your level of how your overall confidence in pursuing your career goal has changed thanks to your pal, Mistress Karen.

Think about how you've changed in the last month: Are you getting along better with colleagues and higher ups—and your paramour—because of your new improved Master Mentality thought processes? Are you more confident about asking people around you to perform job duties that you now can recognize as NOT being part of your 20 percent productivity plan? Is your schedule more balanced? Your confidence level more even

keeled? Are you more relaxed about making day-to-day decisions—as well as more assured in the long-term decision you are
making to pursue your fantasy career goal?

Hopefully, none of these questions are horrifically painful to
answer, because they aren't meant to be. Although I may come
from The Dominatrix School of Higher Learning, I still would
not want you to torture yourself too greatly because you feel that
after our 30 days together you still haven't reached perfection.

Relax.

Trust me. None of us is ever 100 percent perfect—except for
maybe George Clooney, who I'd love to personally whip into
yielding submission, or, if so be it, let him be the the whip-
meister. I know, I know, all you loyal readers out there may wonder why I haven't mentioned Andy Garcia even once as a perfect
specimen, since I was so enthralled with him in my last book. It's
because I've since found out that, alas, Andy suffers from a fatal
character flaw: having a wife.

Speaking of love and marriage (isn't it nice to see those two
words in the same sentence?), one of my favorite authors, Tom
Robbins, once gave the following advice to aspiring spouse
hunters and huntresses:

"We spend all our time looking for the perfect lover when we
should be looking for the perfect love."

The same advice applies to your job. No job is going to be
absolutely perfect. You must accept that now. What you should
be honing in on instead is trying to find a job that is perfect for
you—meaning the dynamic between it and you should be the
thing you should be looking to perfect.

For instance, I accept right now that being a writer comes
with its share of problems—but my passionate, soul-fulfilling
love for writing keeps me pushing forward and upward.

Though I must admit, I often wonder what my life would be
like if I hadn't ultimately quit my advertising career and chosen
instead to become the master of my destiny and pursue my passion for writing. Believe me, it hasn't been the easiest career

path, but it's the only one I could have taken to get me to where I needed to be going—to a place where I was living each day growing, learning, and being challenged (which are all euphemisms for "facing lots of rejection and doubts that ultimately strengthened my character and sense of self—my truest-to-myself-sense-of-self rather than some superficial sense of self that comes from a hoity-toity title and cushy expense account").

Which reminds me of yet another quote about love relationships—this one comes from Woody Allen. How odd, I know, to be quoting Woody of all folks as a relationship expert—but he does assert the following insight:

"As I got more and more successful, I didn't always do better with women. I just got rejected by a higher level of them."

Same will go for you and your career. As you climb higher up the career ladder, you will still face your share of problems—just higher levels of problems.

Many of you may wonder why I'm choosing to end this book on such a *non*-ra-ra-sis-boom-ba kind of note. Perhaps you think I should be saying stuff about how the perfect career life can be found right around the corner, in between a Kinkos and a Starbucks. But I feel it's better for all of us—Mistress Karen included—to remain realistic about life. And real life will always have its share of struggle and pain. You must accept this now, or your career will give you a surprise whipping, instead of the other way around.

It's like this. If you don't accept that Good Humor trucks exist, then you run the risk of being run over by a Good Humor truck. The same goes for all those Bad Humor trucks that are out there. And they are out there, too, bringing with them all sorts of tempting indulgences like anger, cynicism, and regret (see the full menu list above for the other 25). But, thankfully, with the help of this book you will now be better able to deal with each of these things as they each come up and at you.

Yes, although this book may look as if it's over, it's not. You've only just begun to use the information you've received.

In other words: *If you wanna get what you wanna get, then you gotta keep on keeping on.*

You must bring everything you've learned throughout this book into your career life with you on a daily basis.

And a weekly basis.

And monthly.

And yearly.

And lifetimely.

Then (depending upon your faith) next lifetimely.

Mistress Karen suggests (aka: commands) you to use this book FOR AT LEAST ANOTHER THREE MONTHS, just to whip the messages in it fully into you. Meaning? Whenever you feel a negative emotion start to beat you down at the office, whip it into subservience by reading the appropriate chapter in this book.

Feeling cynical? Regretful? Guilty? Consult these chapters.

And if you're ever feeling like you want to procrastinate, then consult me personally. Write me a letter. I'd love to hear from you, and find out what you thought of this book—and how it might have helped you to whip what at first seemed unwhippable. Also, tell me what you liked (and didn't) about this book. I always want to be learning and growing. Actually I always want to be eating or having incredible sex. But other than that, I'll take some learning and growing.

And I wish YOU all four of these as well as you move forward on your search to hunt down—and whip into surrender—your long-term career goal.

All of which reminds me of a good, inspiring Buddhist fable:

Painless Pain

A woman approached a guru and told him she wanted to study under him. He took her under his auspices and each day he'd give her tons of books to read and at the end of the day he'd ask how her studies were going. "Have you learned everything there is to learn?" he'd ask. "No," she'd say, and the guru would clunk her on top of her head with his cane. This exact interaction went on for months and months until one day the guru came in, asked his same question, she again said no—but this time she grabbed the cane from his hand before he could give her a clunk. She nervously awaited his reaction, fearful of his recompense. Instead, he smiled at her and congratulated her, saying, "You now know everything there is to know." She looked back at him confused. The guru explained, "You have learned that you will never learn everything and you have learned how to stop the pain."

Good luck in your search for your ideal long-term career fantasy—and for dealing with all the inevitable obstacles in your path to attaining it.

Happy whipping.